SIZZLE ... E ... E ... W

TH... OGY OF HEA... ENERGY

LIGHT AND SHADOWS · 2
Principles · Make your own sundial · How tall is that tree? · Playing with shadows · Shadow puppet theatre · Light travels in straight lines · Make your own light-ray box · Make your own periscope · Make your own kaleidoscope · Spoon mirrors · Mystery money · Near and far · Telescopes · Splitting white light · Colour spinners · Make your own spectrum · Mixing with light · Separating colours · Seeing red

CHEMICAL ENERGY · 16
Principles · Candle snuffer · Does all air burn? · Fire fighting · Growing · Rotting

PHYSICS OF HEAT · 22
Principles · Keeping warm · Raising your cap · Puddle watching · Convection currents · Heat conductors · Spiral snake · Radiated heat

SOURCES OF ENERGY · 28
Principles · Make your own windmill · Future energy · Nuclear fission · Nuclear fusion

Simon & Schuster Young Books
Wolsey House
Wolsey Road
Hemel Hempstead
Herts HP2 4SS

Design:
David West
Children's Book Design
Editor:
Diana Russell
Illustrations:
Alex Pang and Rob Shone

A CIP catalogue record for this book is available from the British Library

ISBN: 0 7500 0867 9

Printed in Hong Kong
by Wing King Tong Co. Ltd.

SIMON & SCHUSTER

LONDON • SYDNEY • NEW YORK • TOKYO • SINGAPORE • TORONTO

LIGHT AND SHADOWS

Our Earth seems a very large place. But it is only a small planet and it is a tiny scrap compared to the Sun. The Sun looks small because it is about 150 million kilometres away, but without it there could be no Earth. The Sun gives us warmth, light and life. All the energy that is stored in food and fuel came originally from the Sun.

The burning Sun
The Sun is the star at the centre of our solar system. It is a huge ball of glowing gas with a diameter of 1,400,000 km. (Earth's diameter is 12,750 km), yet compared with some stars our Sun is only a dwarf star.

Mirrors and reflection
Light travels in straight lines. It can be bounced back or reflected by mirrors of silvered glass, polished metal or smooth surfaces that reflect light.

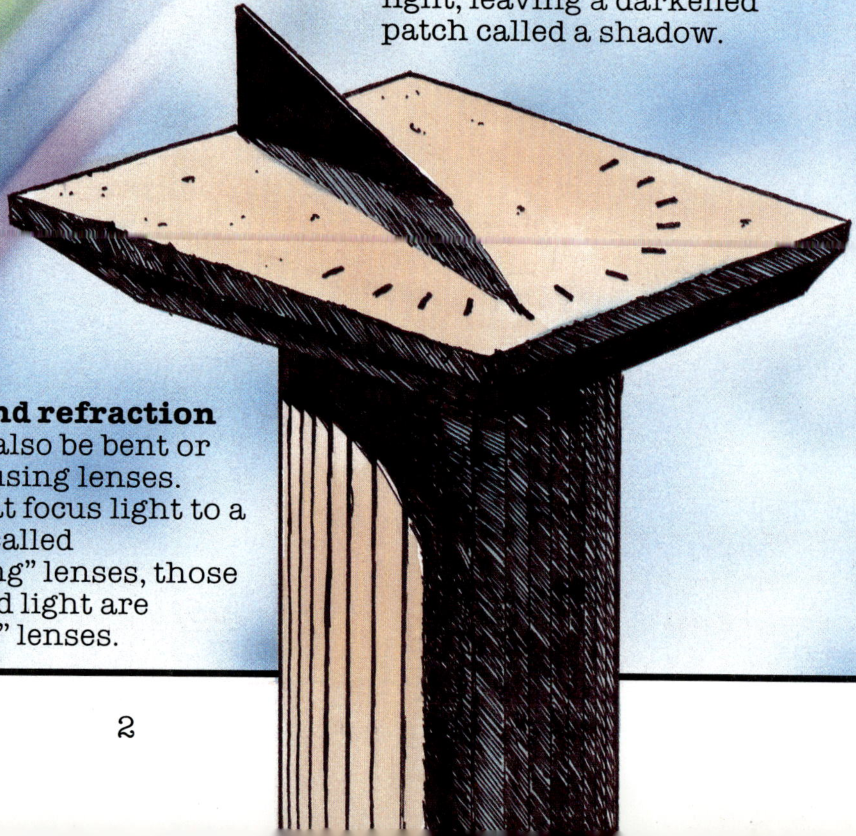

Shadows
When a solid object lies in the path of a beam of light, blocking the light, the object is called "opaque". Opaque objects stop the light, leaving a darkened patch called a shadow.

Lenses and refraction
Light can also be bent or refracted using lenses. Lenses that focus light to a point are called "converging" lenses, those that spread light are "diverging" lenses.

Light and colour
We see colours when light shines on things. It is hard to make out colours in the dark, as very little light is reflected from them into our eyes.

PRINCIPLES OF LIGHT

What is light?
We see when light reflects off things into our eyes. Light is a form of energy called electromagnetic radiation, made up of electrically charged particles. The total spectrum of radiation includes X-rays, ultra violet rays, infra red and radio waves. They each have a different wavelength, or speed of vibration (frequency). Our eyes only react to a very small group of wavelengths that makes visible light.

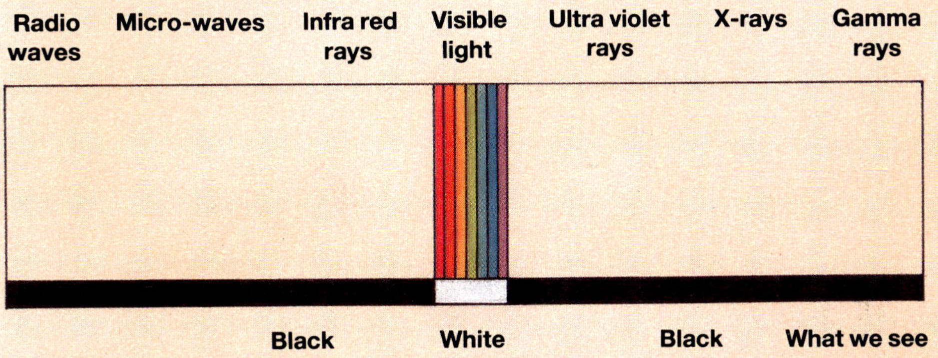

The Sun's energy
Light from the Sun is a mixture of seven colours that we see as white light. Huge amounts of heat and light energy are produced from nuclear reactions deep inside the Sun. Temperatures on the surface can reach 6000 degrees Celsius (°C).

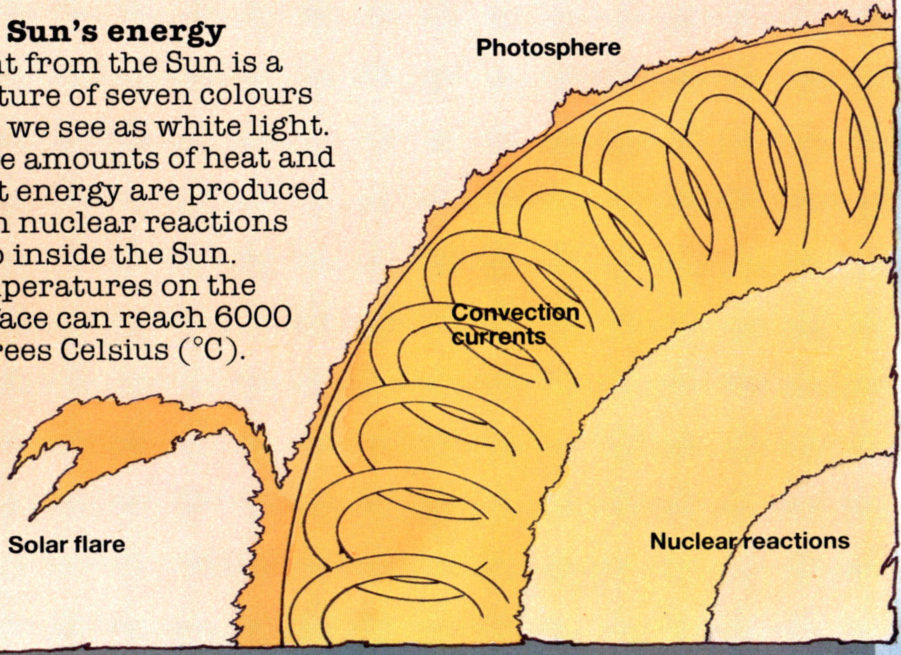

MAKE YOUR OWN SUNDIAL

Set up your sundial on a window sill in a south-facing room early in the morning. You will need a watch and a pen. When your watch shows a whole hour (like 8 a.m.), draw a line passing through the centre of the pencil's shadow and write the time beside it. Do this every hour, on the hour, until late into the afternoon. Notice how the length of the shadow changes during the day.

Any shadow lines missed because the Sun was hidden by cloud can be added on another day. Once marked with the hours, your sundial will show the time whenever the Sun shines.

HOW TALL IS THAT TREE?

You can find the height of a tree with a metre-long stick and shadows. Use the stick to measure the length of the tree's shadow, to the nearest metre. Measure the stick's shadow to the nearest decimetre. Use a calculator to divide the length of the tree's shadow by the length of the stick's shadow to give the tree's height. If a tree's shadow is 12 metres and the stick's shadow is 1.5 metres, the tree's height is 8 metres (12 divided by 1.5).

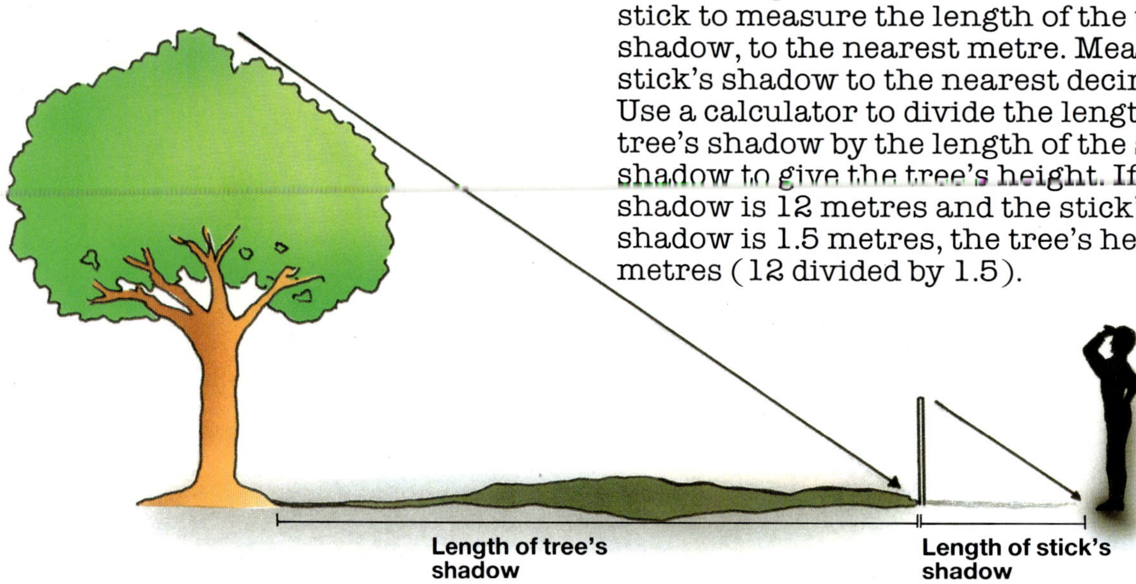

PLAYING WITH SHADOWS

Look for your shadow on a bright, sunny day. Can you run away and leave it behind? Shadow box with a friend's shadow, without touching each other. Use a torch or table lamp in a dark room to make shadows on a wall. Watch what happens to their size if you move things towards or away from the light.

Hand shadows
Try making animal shapes with your hands, like a bird that flaps its wings. Use your finger tips to make the head of a dog.

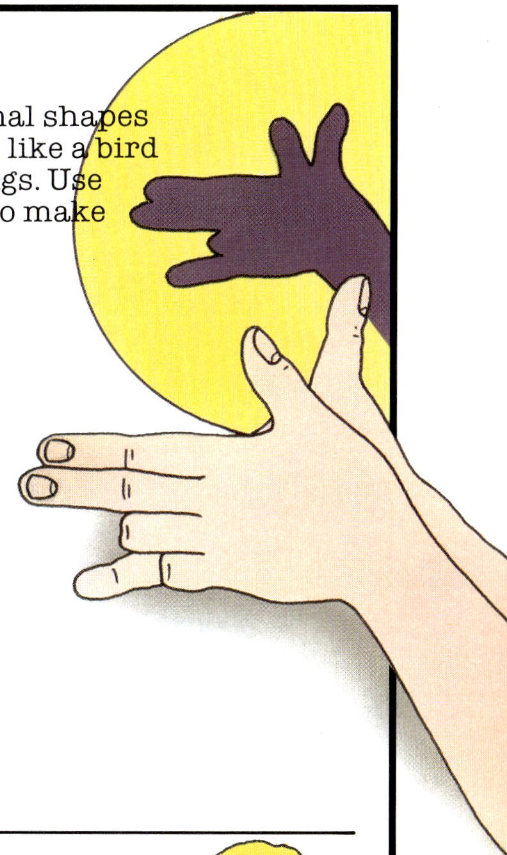

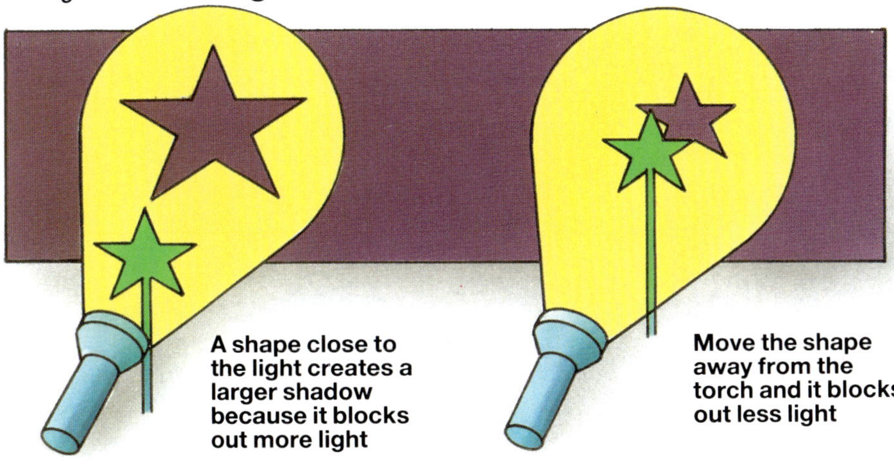

SHADOW PUPPET THEATRE

Use a lamp to light up a screen made from an old cotton sheet or table cloth. Carefully cut out scenery and character shapes from card. Pin the scenery to the sheet. Tape your characters to thin sticks, like garden canes, so they can move across the screen. Make up a play to entertain your friends and family. You can make your shadow puppets even more realistic by having moving parts held together with paper fasteners.

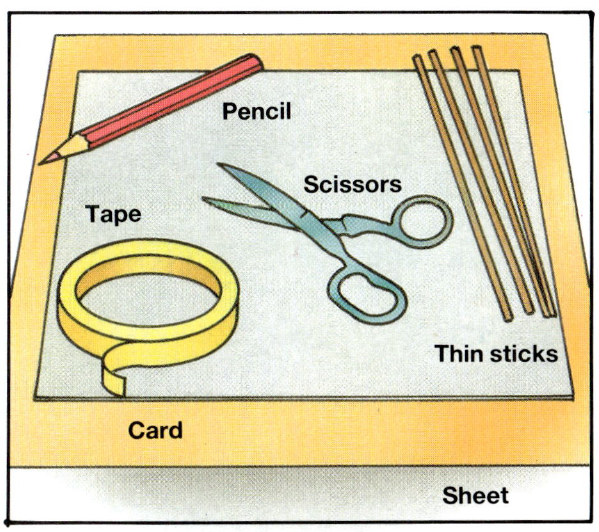

LIGHT TRAVELS IN STRAIGHT LINES

You can show that light travels in a straight line if you put a tiny light, like a small bulb or a candle, at one end of a table. (Stand a candle in a tray full of sand or set securely on a saucer.) Make a small hole in a square of card and set the card in modelling clay so that you can see the light through the hole. Line up the hole in a second card so that you can still see the bulb or flame. Set up a third card, too, so that you can see the light through all three holes. Always blow out the candle after your investigation.

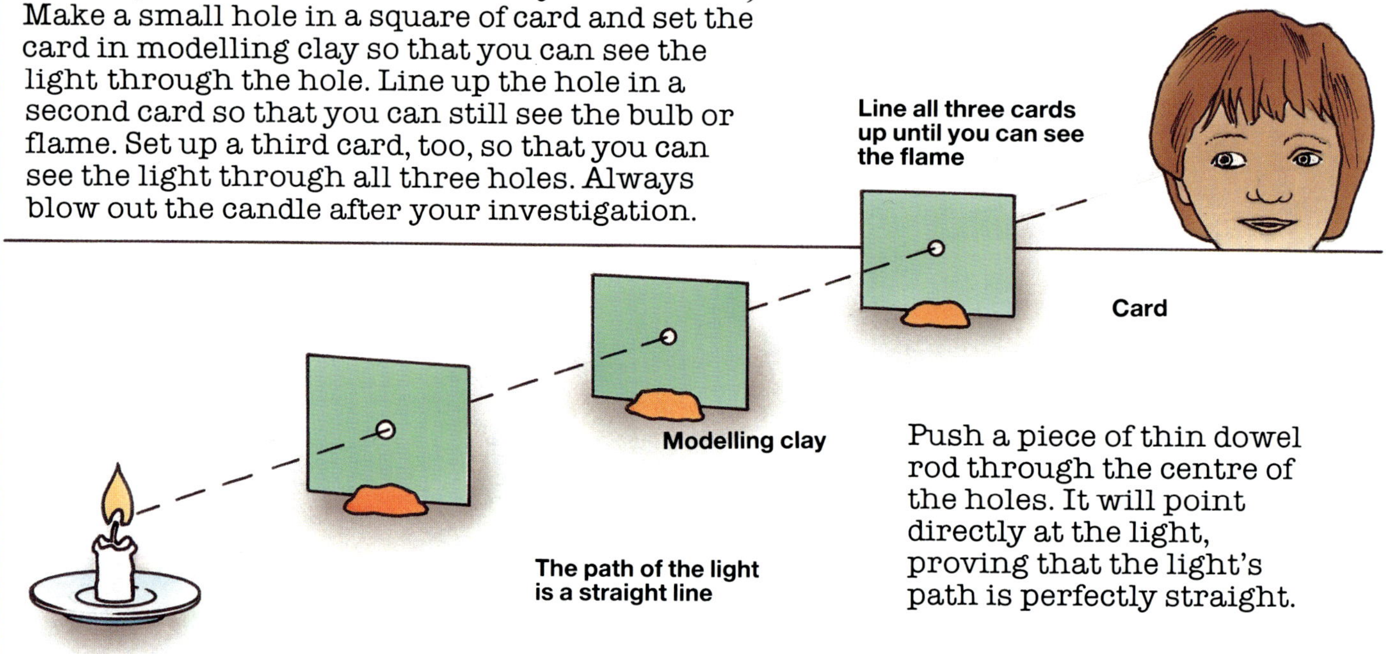

Push a piece of thin dowel rod through the centre of the holes. It will point directly at the light, proving that the light's path is perfectly straight.

MAKE YOUR OWN LIGHT-RAY BOX

Many interesting experiments can be done using a light box. The light from a torch shines through the slit in the box. Put your light box on a table in a darkened room and set a mirror in front of it. Watch how the angle between the light beam and its reflection changes as you move the mirror.

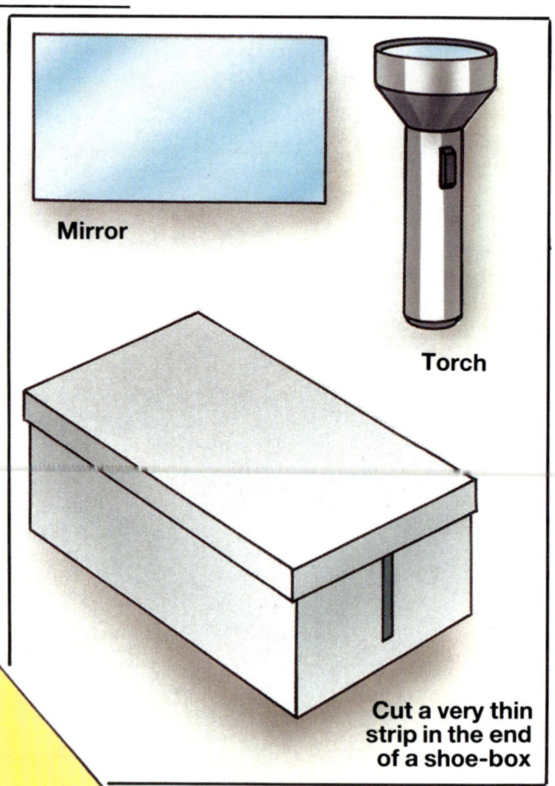

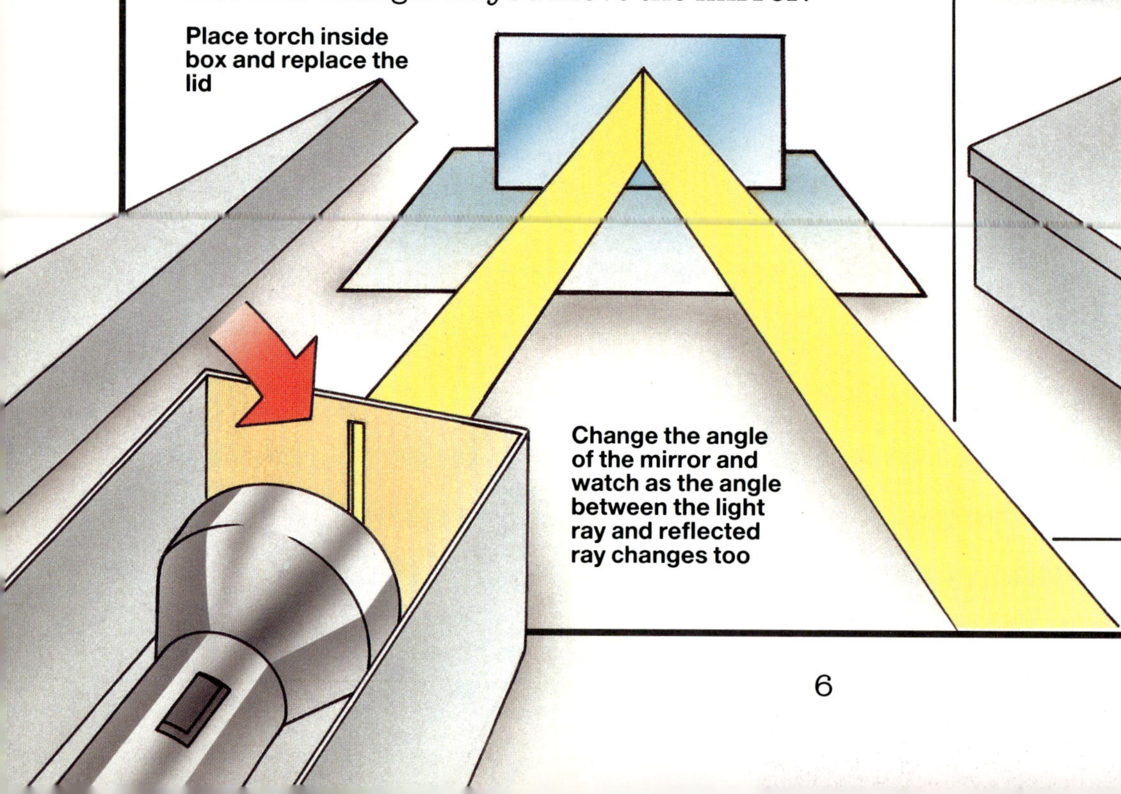

MAKE YOUR OWN PERISCOPE

Can you see round a corner or over a wall without being seen? Submarines use periscopes to see what is above them without having to come to the surface. You can make a periscope from card with slits cut into the sides to take two small mirrors. You must set the angle of the mirror slits at 45° (half a right angle), so that the light will be reflected through the periscope tube.

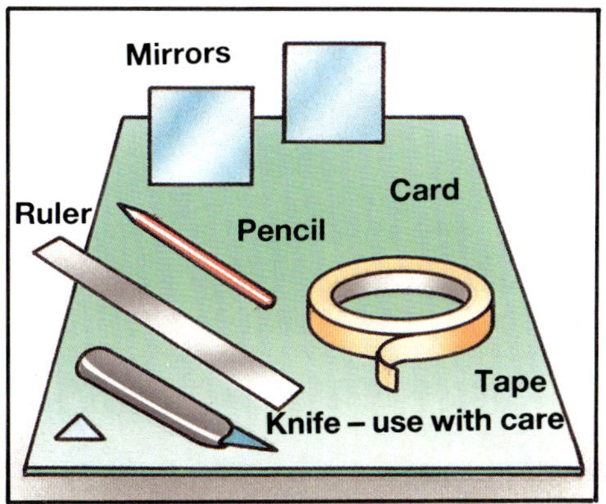

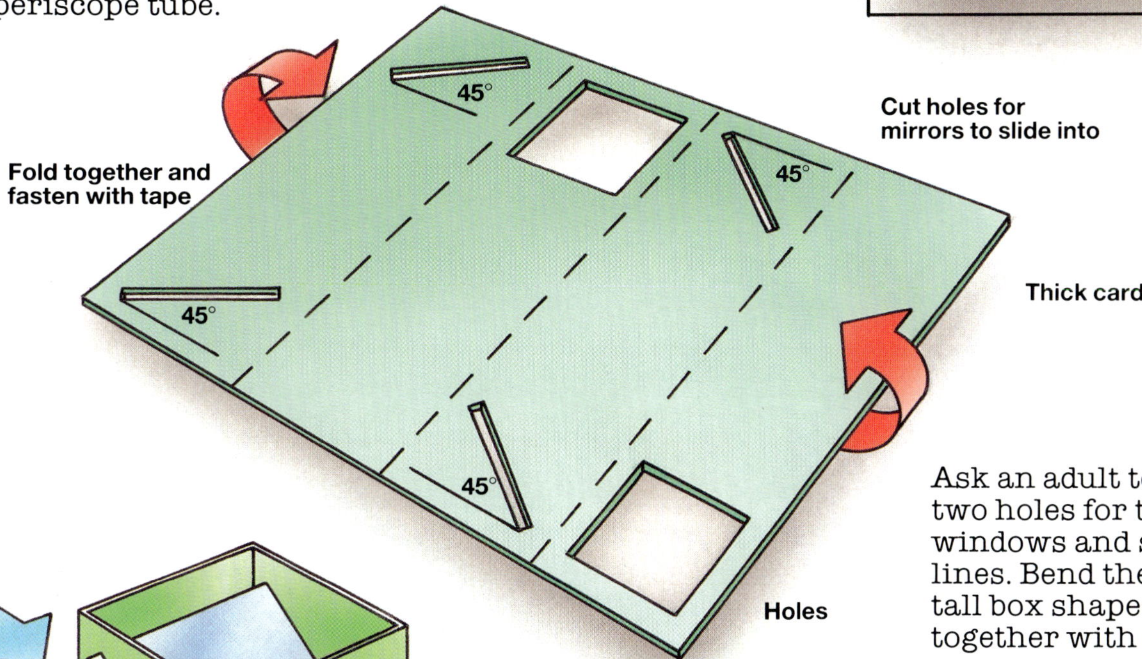

Ask an adult to cut out the two holes for the viewing windows and score the fold lines. Bend the card into a tall box shape. Hold it together with tape.

How it works
Light, reflected from an object, enters through the top window and is reflected off the top mirror. The angle of the mirror sends the light down to the bottom mirror. This reflects the light out through the bottom window and into your eyes.

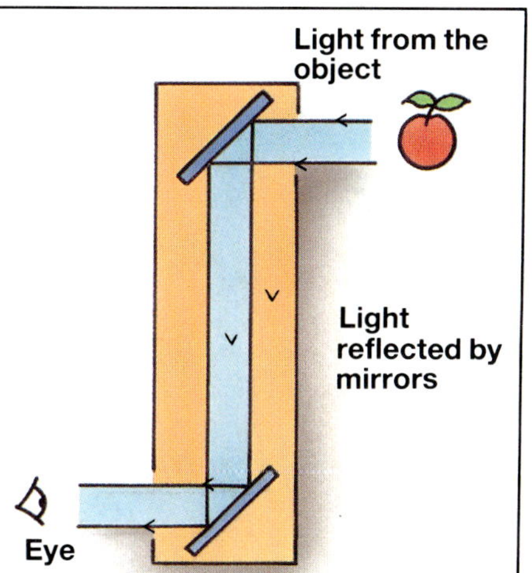

MAKE YOUR OWN KALEIDOSCOPE

Kaleidoscopes are very old toys that use mirrors to produce colourful, changing patterns. You can make your own by taping together three small mirrors into a triangle. Hold the mirrors over a collection of small beads or brightly coloured tissue paper scraps and look down inside the mirrors. To change the pattern, find a transparent dish or jar that the mirrors can stand in. Hold the dish and the mirrors up, so that light can shine in through the bottom, and slowly turn the dish as you look down. The effect is even better if you can hold your kaleidoscope at an angle so that the beads move inside the mirrors.

Multiple reflections

Tape two small mirrors together and stand them on a table top. Place a small toy between them and count the number of reflections that you can see. Make the angle larger, by moving the mirrors apart. Is the number of reflections more or less? Now move the mirrors closer together. Watch what happens to the number of reflections.

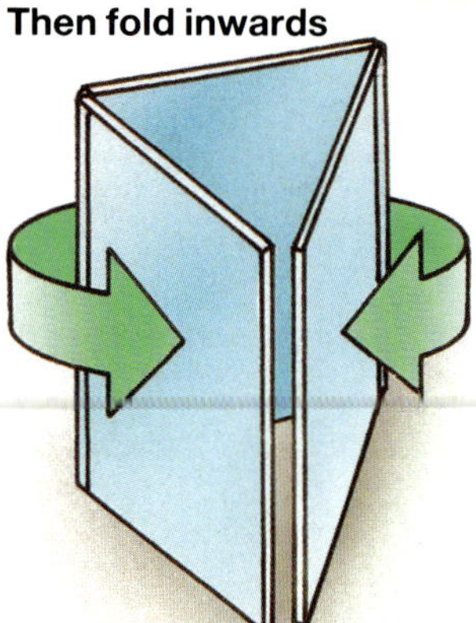

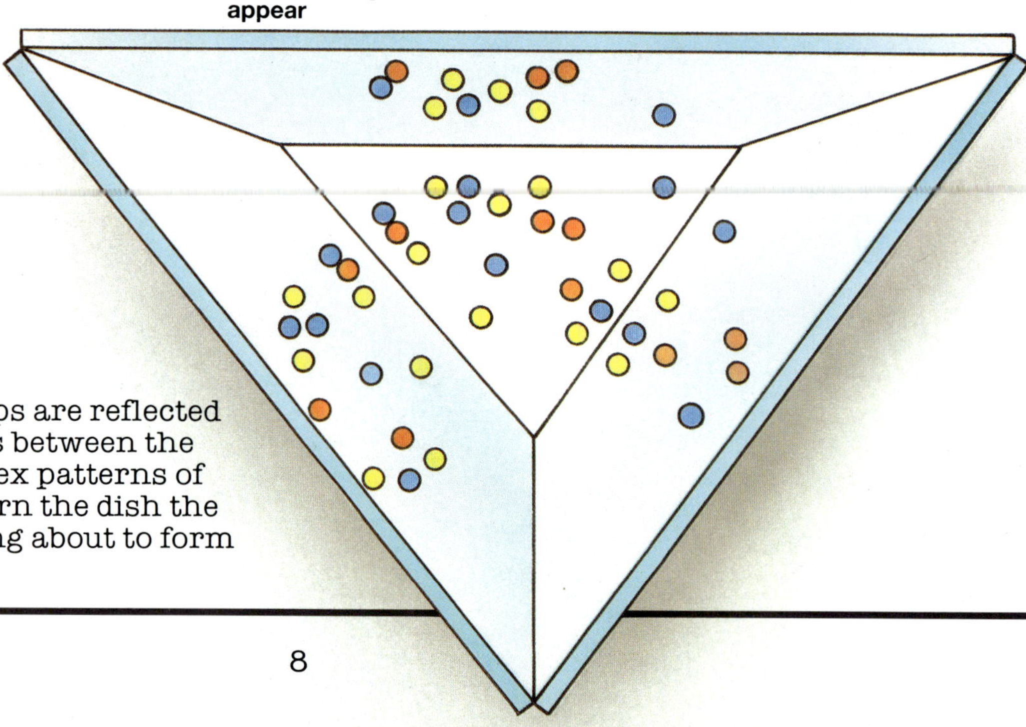

The beads or tissue scraps are reflected backwards and forwards between the mirrors, building complex patterns of coloured light. As you turn the dish the beads roll around, moving about to form new patterns.

SPOON MIRRORS

Have you ever been to a fairground hall of mirrors? The strangely shaped mirrors make you look very odd indeed. Any bendy mirror will distort or alter your shape. You may be lucky enough to have a plastic mirror that you can bend gently to change to the shape of your reflection. If not, you can use a large spoon. Look into the bowl of a very shiny spoon. This is like a concave or hollowed out mirror. What is strange about your image? Now turn the spoon around and look at your reflection in the back of the spoon. This is a convex mirror. How do you look now?

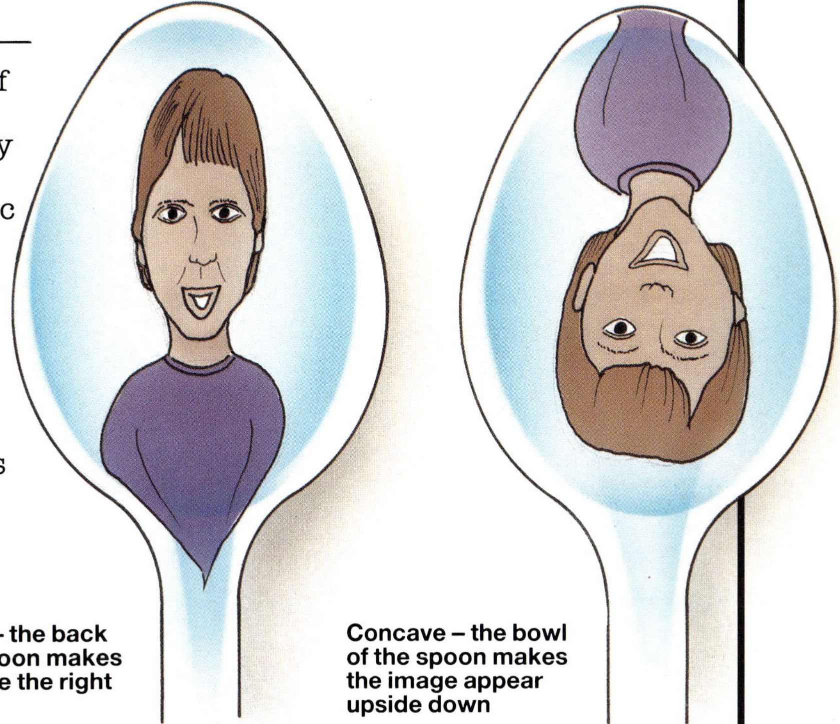

Convex – the back of the spoon makes the image the right way up

Concave – the bowl of the spoon makes the image appear upside down

MYSTERY MONEY

If you look at fish in a pool they seem quite close. When you dip your hand in to touch them you find they are deeper than you thought. Your eyes are being fooled by an illusion created by the water. Light rays bend as they pass from water into air and make you think that the water is shallower than it really is.

Bendy pencil
Light rays change direction as they pass from water to air, so any object in water seems to bend. A pencil seems to be bent at the place where it enters the water.

Put a coin in a bowl. Look over the rim, slowly bend down until the coin disappears from view. Get someone to pour water slowly into the bowl. As it fills the coin will reappear.

The light reflected from the coin is bent towards you as it passes from the water into the air. So you can now see the coin, even though the rim hid it before.

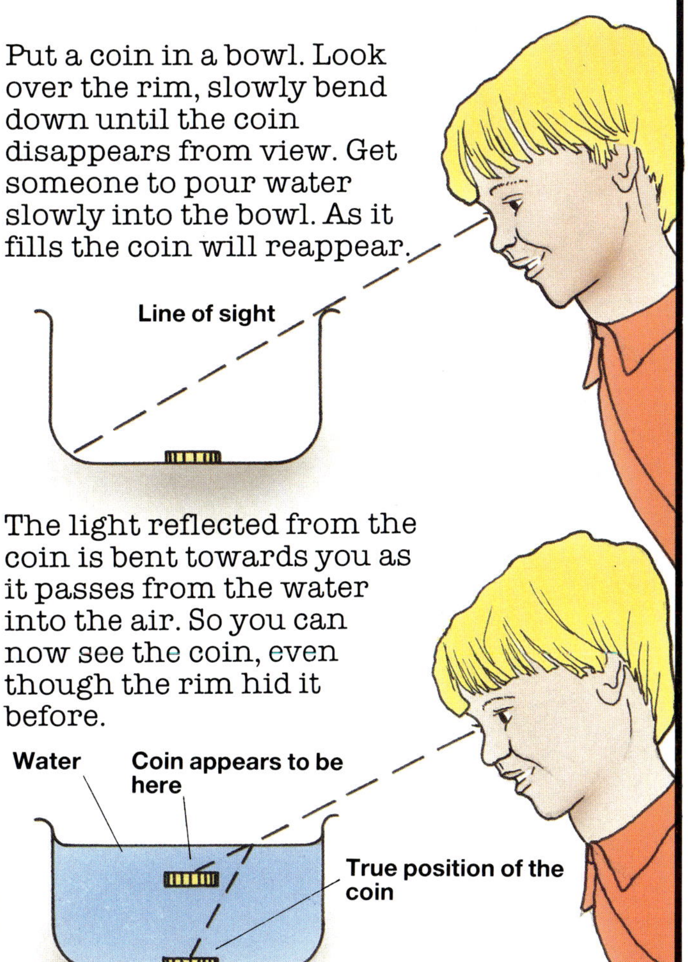

NEAR AND FAR

Lenses bend or refract light, changing the image that we see. Someone who finds it hard to see objects close up (this is called being long-sighted), wears glasses fitted with convex or magnifying lenses to re-focus the light onto the retina at the back of the eyes. People who cannot focus on far-off objects (they are short-sighted), wear glasses with concave lenses. You can see the effects of these different lenses by holding them in the path of a series of light rays shining through slots cut into the end of a shoe-box. Set up the light box in a darkened room and observe how the light rays are bent, or refracted, through the lenses.

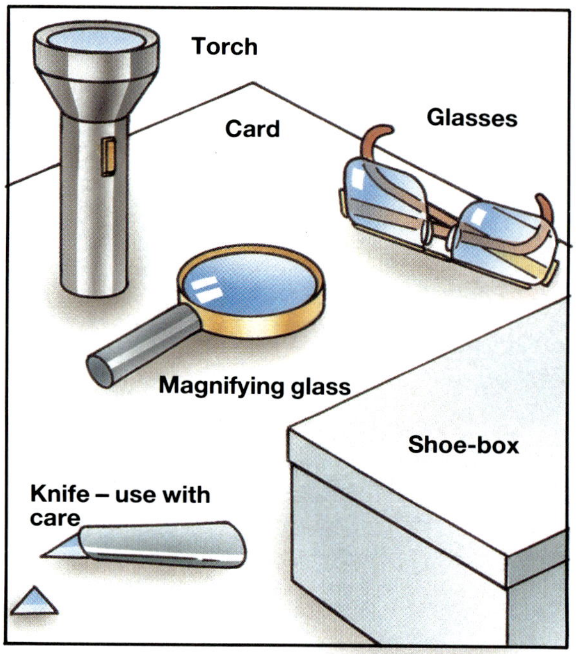

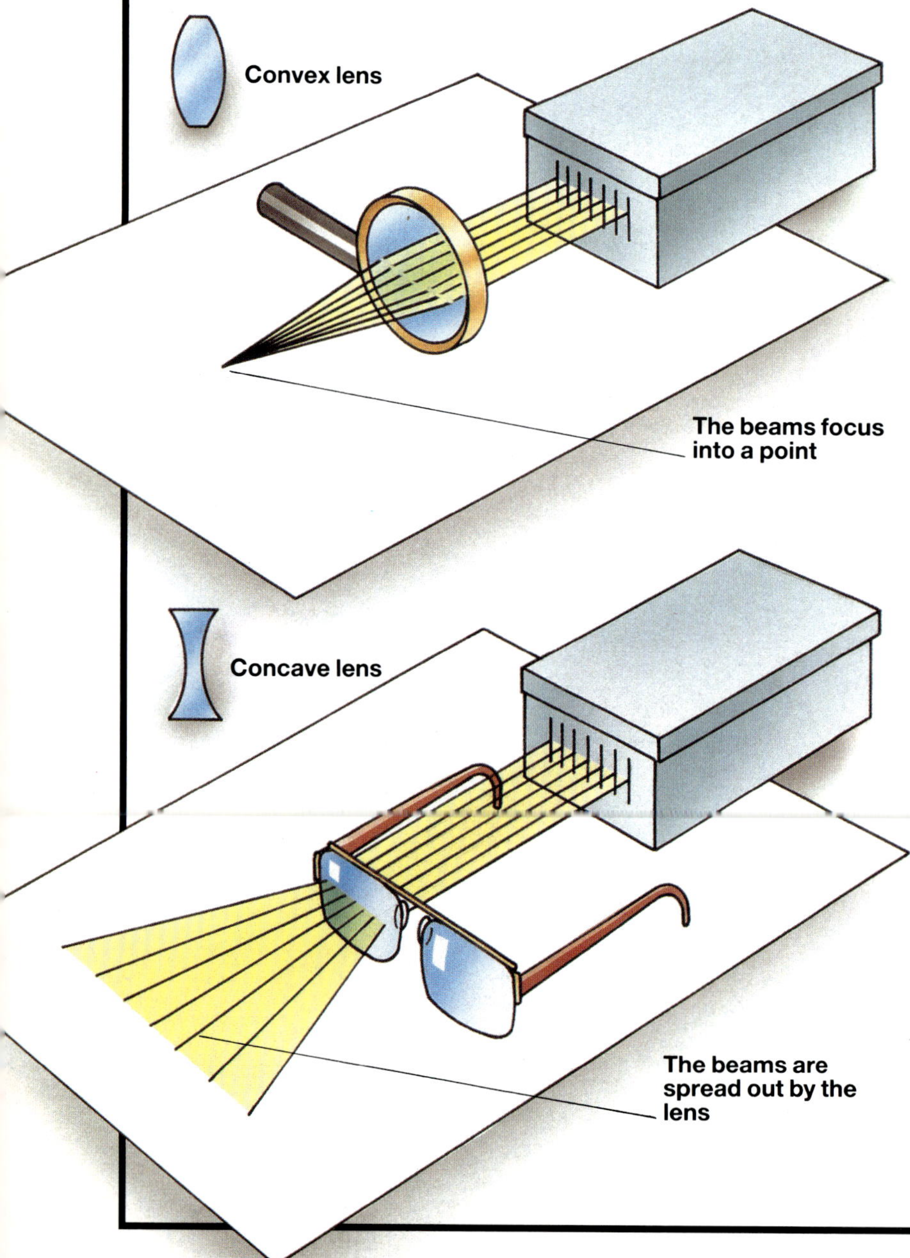

Water drop lens
Water has a "skin" caused by tension in the surface that pulls small drops of water into a rounded shape. Because of this, water drops can act like tiny convex lenses. Put a drop of water on a thin piece of transparent plastic or glass and place it on a picture. You will see the picture seems to be much bigger.

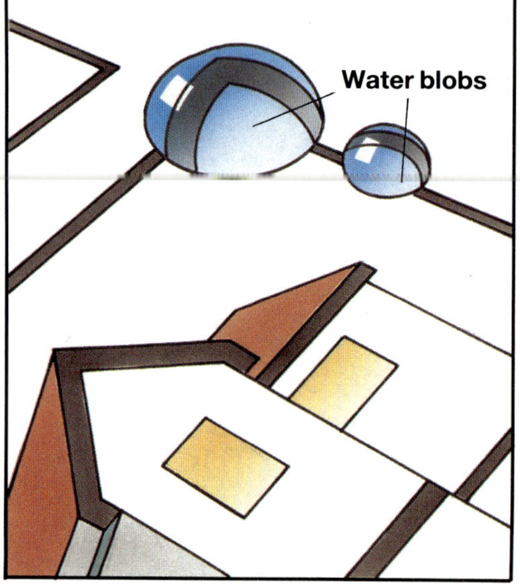

TELESCOPES

People have known for at least 800 years that lenses can magnify objects. The earliest telescopes were made by Flemish lens grinders. These early refracting telescopes (telescopes that use glass lenses to magnify and focus light) did not magnify things very well but an Italian scientist and astronomer named Galileo showed how they could be improved to allow very detailed observations to be made. Reflecting telescopes, invented by the English scientist, Newton, used a concave mirror to collect light from distant objects. As mirrors were easier to make, his reflecting telescopes could be made much larger; which led to further discoveries. Even the radio waves that are produced by distant stars and galaxies can be collected and focused by special dishes that make up radio telescopes. These give valuable information about objects at the very edge of the universe.

Refracting telescopes
A simple refracting telescope can be made with two convex lenses in a tube. More powerful refracting telescopes use many lenses, giving a clearer, sharper image.

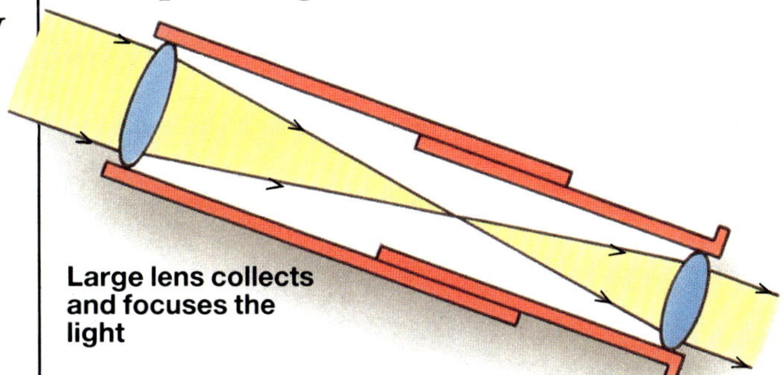

Reflecting telescopes
Instead of a lens, reflecting telescopes use a concave mirror to collect and focus the light. An eyepiece lens increases the magnification of the image.

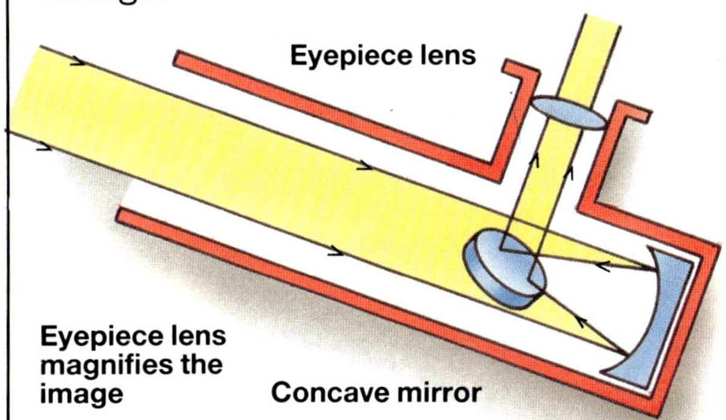

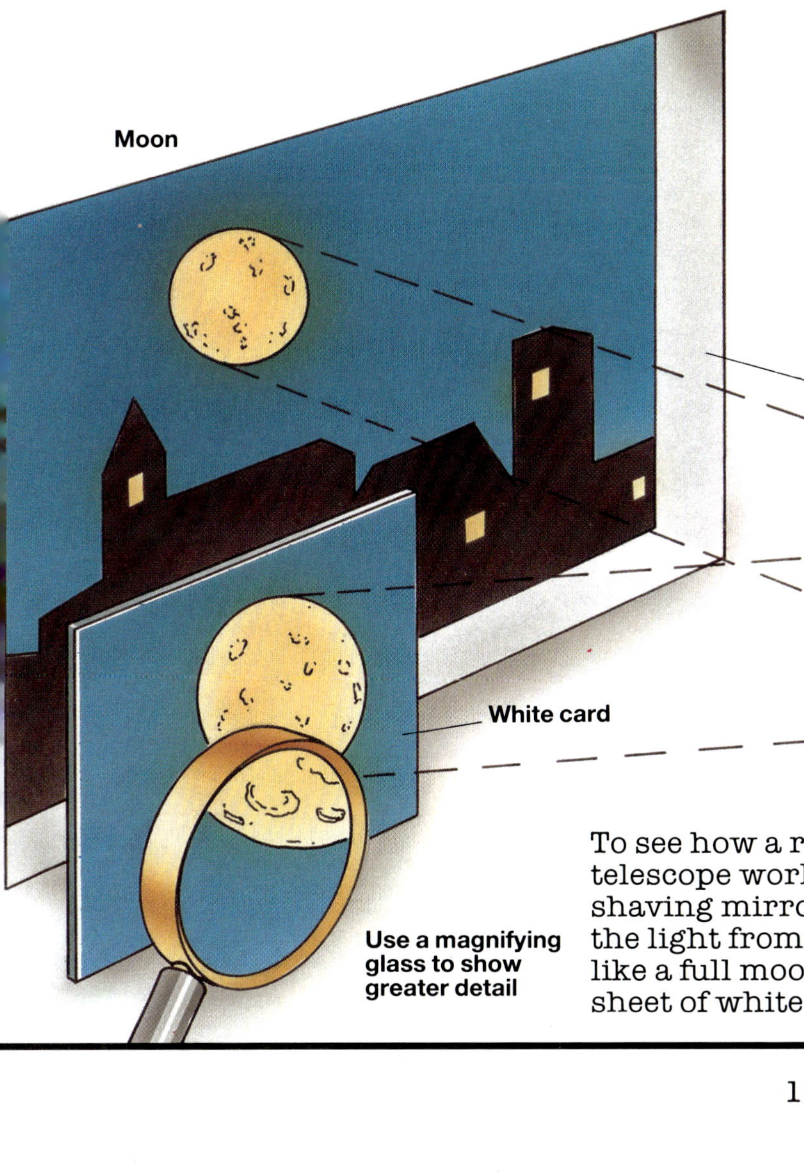

To see how a reflecting telescope works, use a shaving mirror to focus the light from a far object, like a full moon, onto a sheet of white card.

SPLITTING WHITE LIGHT

White light, the light that comes from the Sun, can be split into seven different colours, called the spectrum of visible light, using a glass prism. A ray of light refracted through the glass is divided up into these seven colours because each colour has a different wavelength and so it is bent or refracted through a different angle. The colours are red, orange, yellow, blue, green, indigo and violet.

Sir Isaac Newton
In 1666 Newton discovered that white light is made up of different colours. He used a prism to split a beam of sunlight coming through a slit in a window blind into a darkened room.

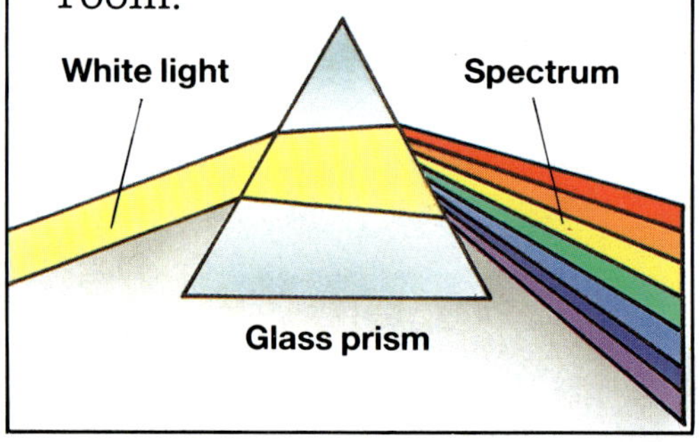

Colours of the rainbow
If the Sun is behind you and rain in front of you, the raindrops refract the sunlight, which splits into the spectral colours, forming a rainbow.

Hose pipe rainbow
On a sunny day, adjust the nozzle on a hose pipe to make a fine mist of water. Stand with your back to the Sun and spray the water into the air. You will see a rainbow in the mist of water droplets.

COLOUR SPINNERS

Mixing light is very different from mixing paint. The more colours of paints or pigments that are mixed together, the darker the mixture becomes. This is called subtractive colour mixing. When light of different colours is mixed, the lighter it becomes. This is called additive colour mixing. Light reflected from colour spinners mixes in this way. To see this for yourself, use a cup to draw circles on pieces of white card and carefully cut these out. Push a pencil stub through the centre of each spinner disc. (Short pencil stubs are easier to spin.) Colour the discs with paints or felt-tipped pens, dividing each disc into seven equal areas and colouring each area with a different colour of the spectrum. Then set the discs spinning.

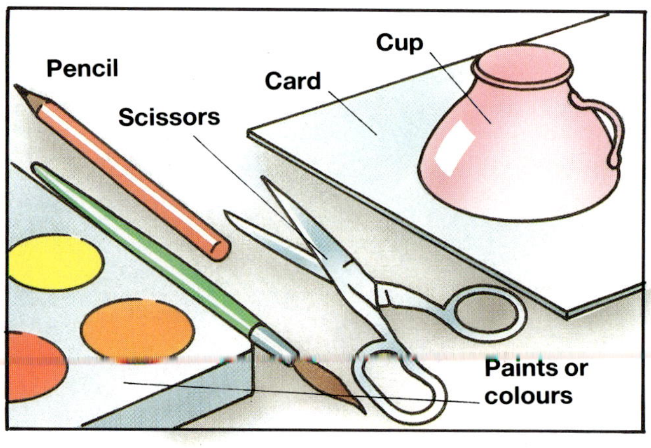

Use cup to draw circle on card and cut out

MAKE YOUR OWN SPECTRUM

Carefully cut a slit into a sheet of card and tape it to a window. Darken the room by pulling the curtains or blinds, letting through only the ray of light from the slit. Reflect the light ray from a mirror lying in a dish of water onto a piece of white card.

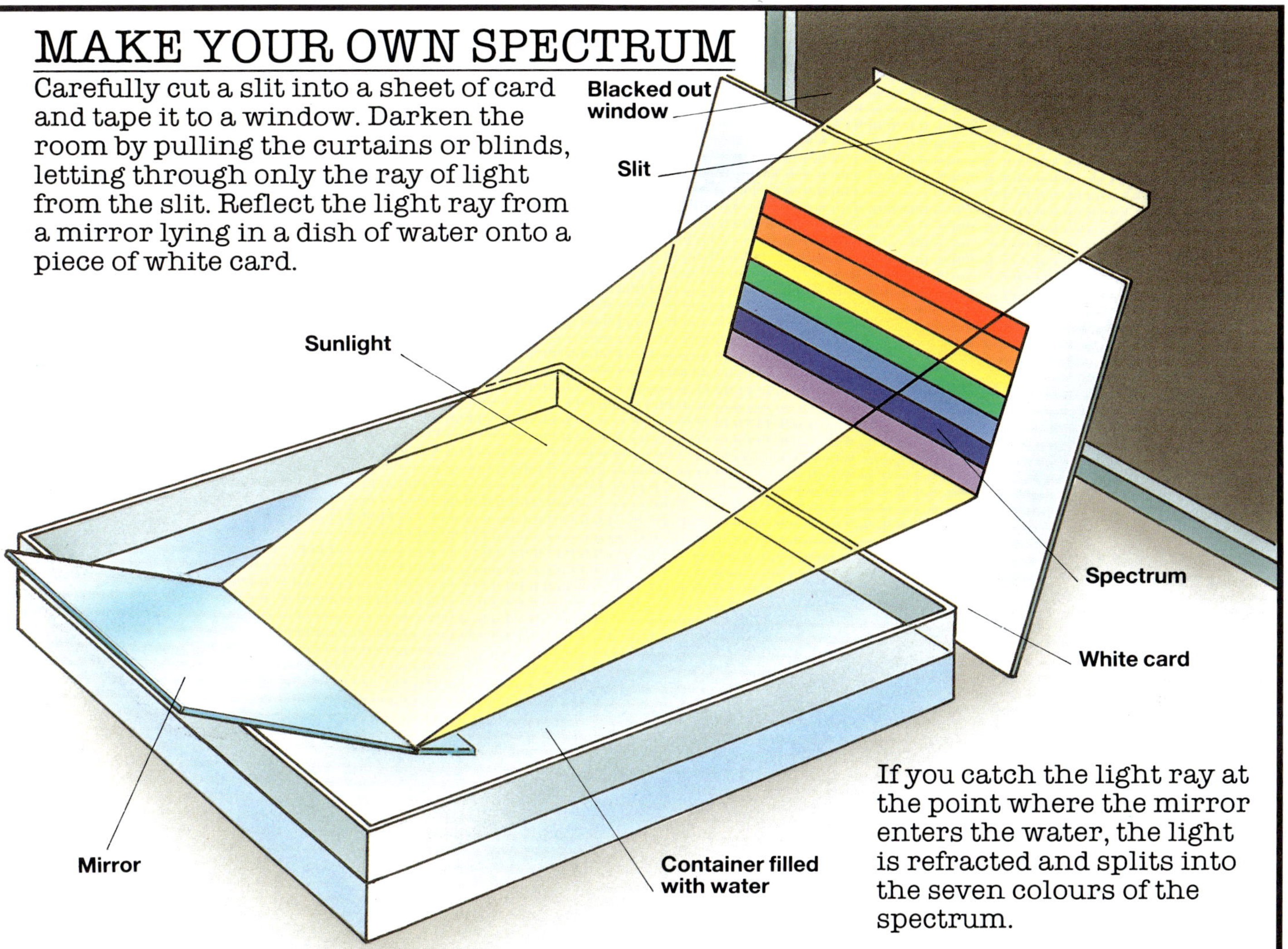

If you catch the light ray at the point where the mirror enters the water, the light is refracted and splits into the seven colours of the spectrum.

You can test the effect of different colour combinations on different spinners.

Because the disc spins so quickly your eyes cannot make out the separate colours and they merge together so that the disc looks grey/white. You can never get a perfect white because the card and paints are not pure colours.

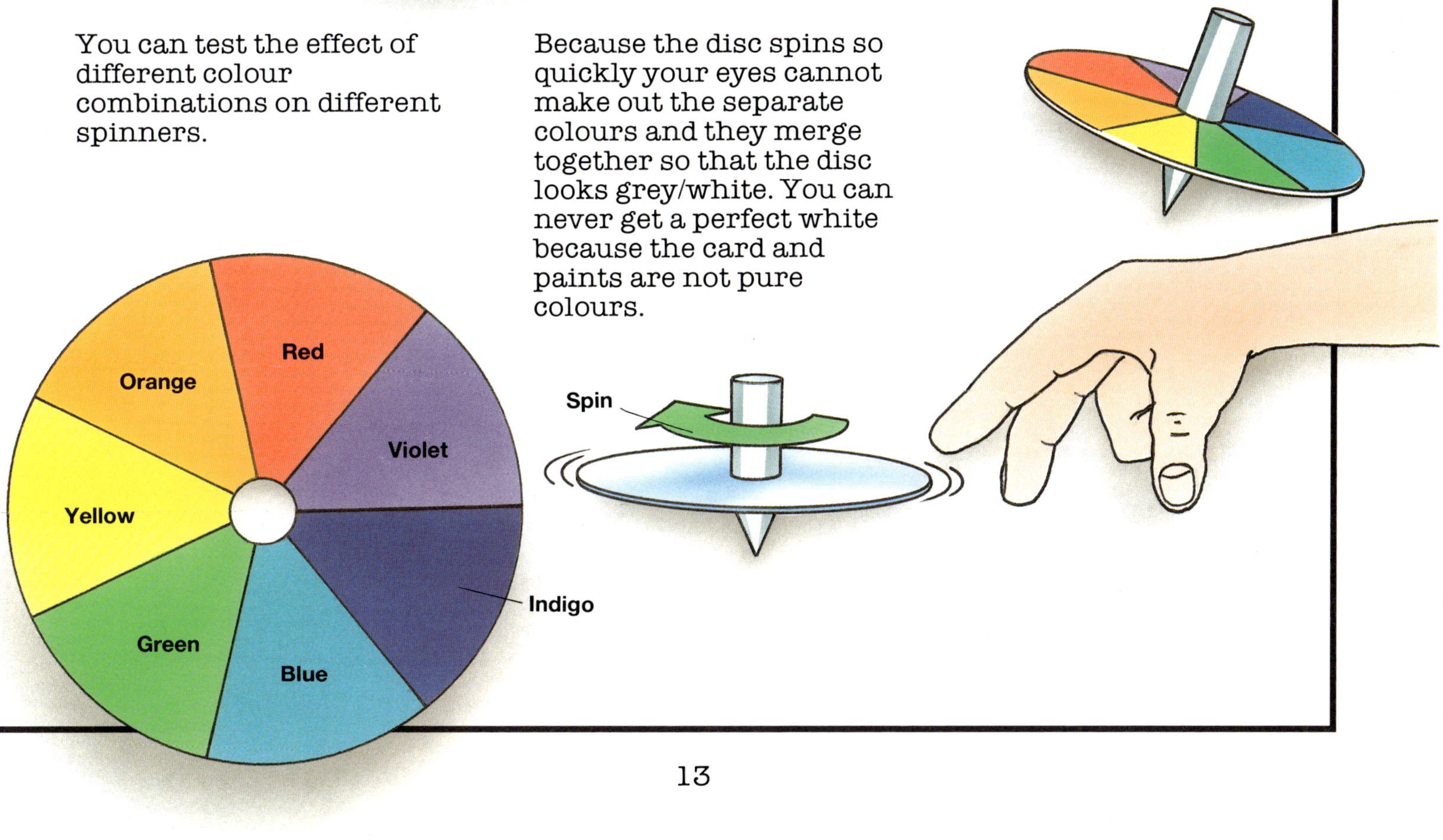

Why we see colour
We see colours because everything around us absorbs white light and reflects back only some of the spectral colours. White objects reflect almost all the spectrum, but black ones absorb them, reflecting back almost no colour at all. Red things absorb spectral colours, reflecting only red light. Blue objects reflect blue light, and so on.

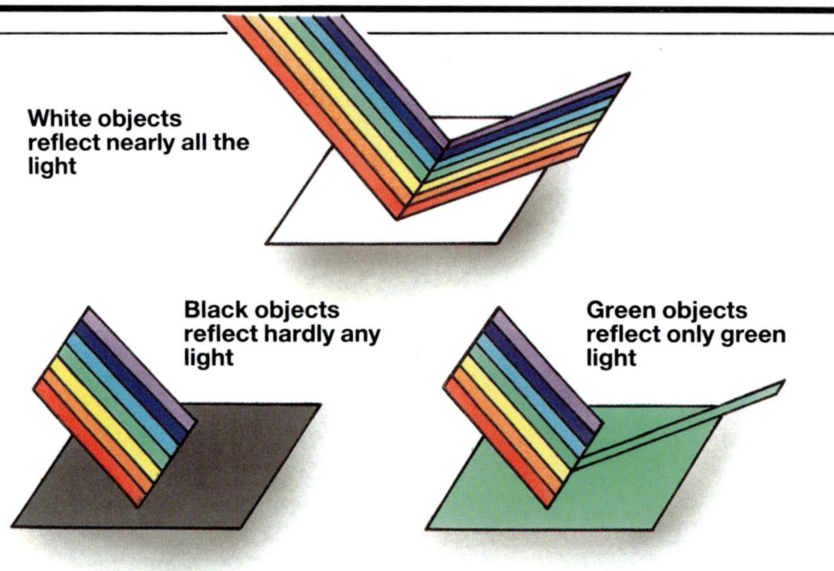

MIXING WITH LIGHT

You can see what happens when coloured light is shone on objects. Ask friends to help you with this experiment. Cover three powerful torches with red, blue and green cellophane or colour filters. Shine all three torches on a sheet of white paper in a very dark room. Look carefully at the way light mixes, it is not like mixing paint. Paints mix to make darker colours, light mixes to make lighter colours. Notice how the colour of objects like your toys changes when you shine coloured light on them.

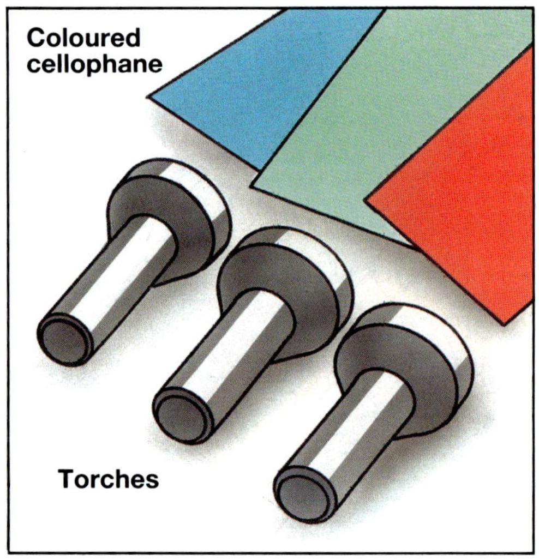

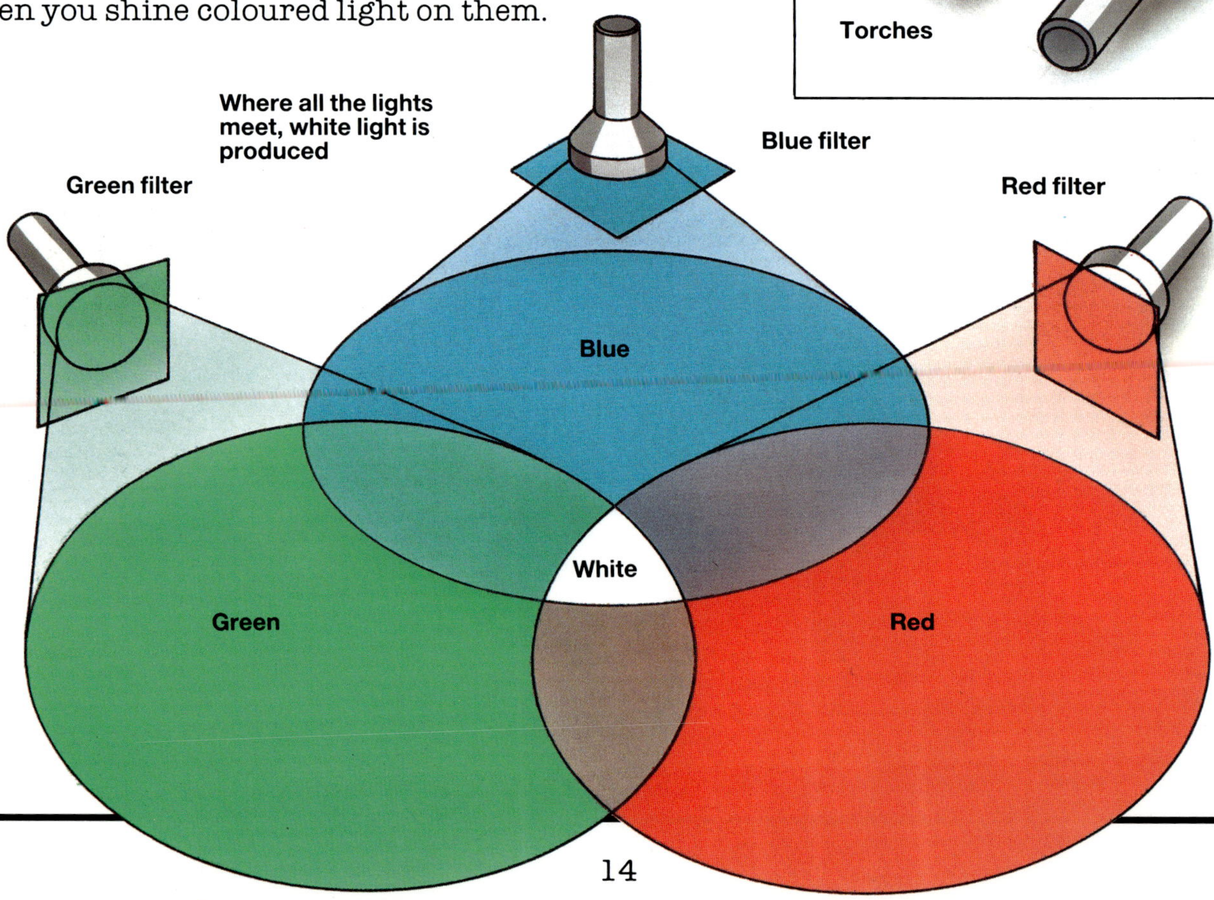

SEPARATING COLOURS

Many colours, such as food dyes and the ink in felt-tipped pens, are mixtures of colours. It is possible to split some colours by a process called chromatography. Put a large spot of one colour at the bottom of a strip of blotting paper. Tape the strip to a pencil and rest it on a jar with some water in it. The water soaks into the blotting paper, carrying the ink with it. The different colours in the ink move at different speeds, so they spread out along the paper.

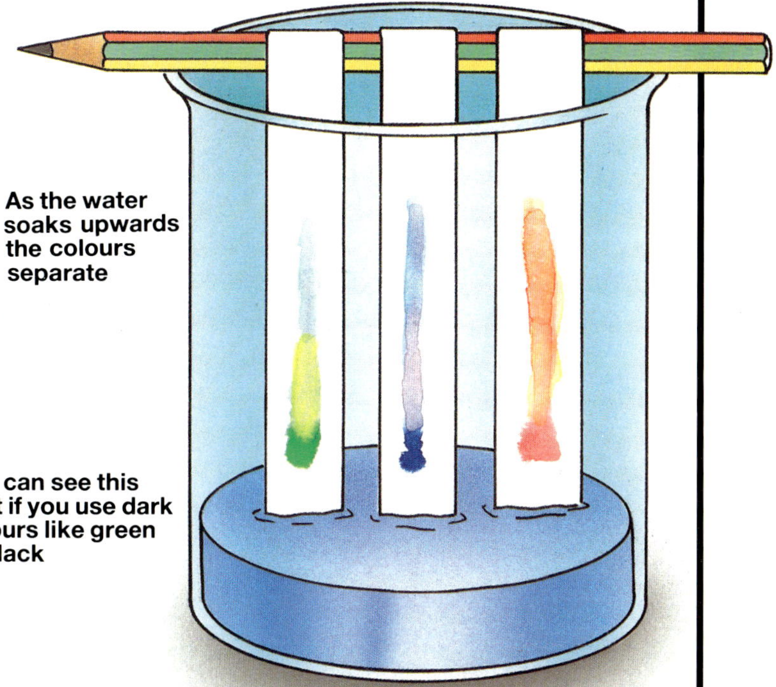

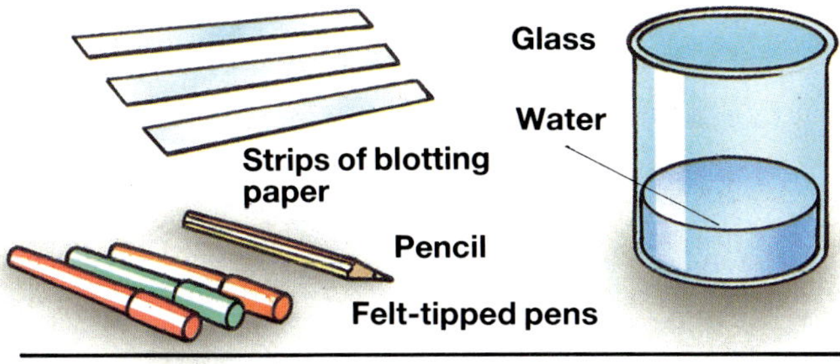

SEEING RED

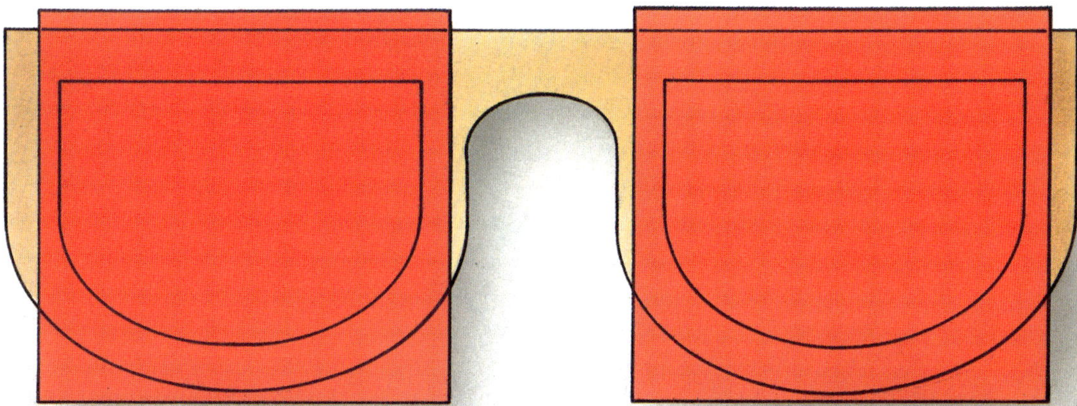

Carefully cut out some card glasses at about the size shown. Find some pieces of coloured cellophane, like sweet wrappers. Any coloured material that you can see through clearly will do. Paste the pieces over the eye holes of your glasses and look at familiar objects. Notice how their colours are changed. Try different coloured cellophane in your glasses. Do you like a yellow world or would you prefer a cool blue one? Do some colours make you feel warm, do others make you happy? Which is your favourite colour?

CHEMICAL ENERGY

Chemical energy is a form of stored energy or fuel. Most chemical energy is released by burning, giving heat and light. Fuel liko oil, gas and coal was formed over millions of years from dead plants and animals. Food is also stored energy. Plants make their own food from sunlight by a process called photosynthesis. Some animals (herbivores) eat plants to get the energy they need to grow. Other animals (carnivores) get their food energy by eating other animals.

Why do we eat?
We eat to get energy. Food is broken down inside our bodies into proteins, vitamins, minerals and so on. This is digestion. It provides all the things we need to keep warm, to grow and to stay healthy.

Solar energy
The Sun gives us all the energy we need, but we cannot live off warmth and sunlight alone. We need food. The Sun makes our food, which gives us our energy.

PRINCIPLES OF CHEMICAL ENERGY

Food chains
Herbivores are animals that eat plants to get the energy they need to live. Other animals, the carnivores, eat the herbivores. When animals die, scavengers such as insects eat the dead tissue. Dead plant material, such as leaf mould and tree bark, forms the food of many fungi. Decayed plant and animal tissue produces minerals to fertilize the land for more plants to grow. Everywhere there are complex food chains of plants and animals living off each other. Each link in the chain gets the energy it needs for life from other plants or animals. Every food chain begins with green plants and the Sun.

The food chain

Oxygen and carbon dioxide
The chemical energy in food that is essential for life can only be released in the body's cells if oxygen is present there as well. All animals need a constant supply of oxygen, breathed in from the air, so that a complex series of chemical reactions can take place to release the energy. Animals breathe out carbon dioxide as a waste product (something they do not need) of these reactions. Plants take in carbon dioxide, from the air or absorbed in water, to create their own energy. They give out oxygen as a product of photosynthesis, putting the oxygen which animals need back into the atmosphere.

Animals and plants
Animals depend upon plants for their food energy. Animals are energy-consumers; plants are energy-producers, but where do plants get their energy supply?

Photosynthesis
Green plants make energy through a process called photosynthesis. Complex chemical reactions turn carbon dioxide, water and sunlight into energy-rich sugars and oxygen, using a chemical, chlorophyll, that gives leaves their green colour.

CANDLE SNUFFER

A candle burns until its wax has gone, unless it is blown out. It gets its chemical energy from the wax. But it also needs air to make it burn. Put a candle in a tray of sand or soil and ask an adult to light it for you. Put a large glass (not plastic) jar over the candle. When the candle has used up the air in the jar it goes out.

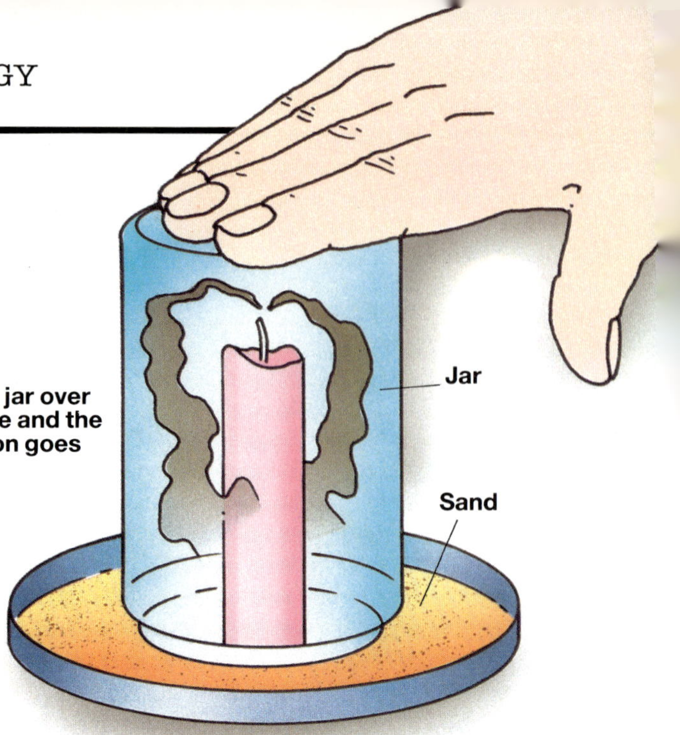

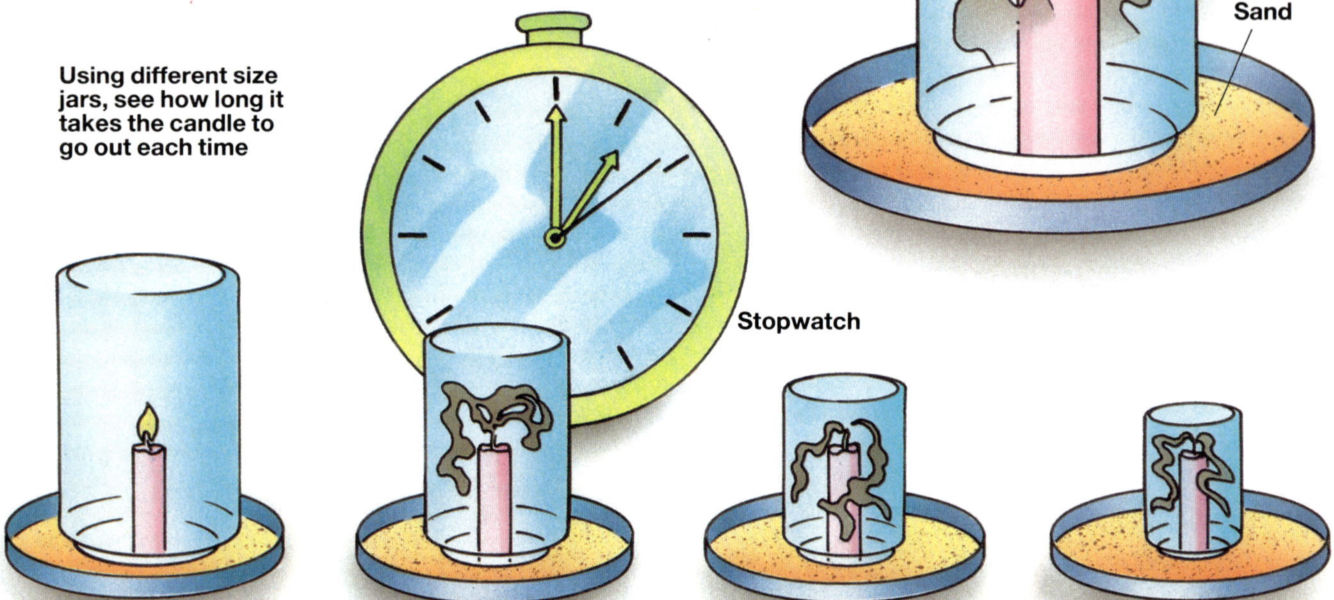

DOES ALL AIR BURN?

Put a candle in a dish of water. Ask an adult to light it. Put a glass jar over it, resting on some coins to keep a gap between the jar and dish. As the candle burns, it uses up part of the air in the jar. The space left by the used up air is filled by water sucked in from the dish, but it only fills about a fifth of the space in the jar.

Air is about four fifths nitrogen, one fifth oxygen, with a tiny amount of carbon dioxide and other gases. Only oxygen burns, so it is the space left by that which is filled by the water.

FIRE-FIGHTING

To put out a fire you must stop oxygen reaching it. Water will drench the fire, so air can't reach it, fire-proof blankets can be thrown over small fires, and foam or carbon dioxide extinguishers will smother a fire in the same way. You can make your own carbon dioxide extinguisher with bicarbonate of soda (baking powder) and vinegar. The baking soda reacts with the acid in vinegar to make carbon dioxide gas. Ask an adult to help you set up a small candle in a sand tray and mix the ingredients in a large beaker. As the mixture froths, hold the beaker above the flame. **DON'T** pour the liquid on the flame, just let the gas flow over the flame.

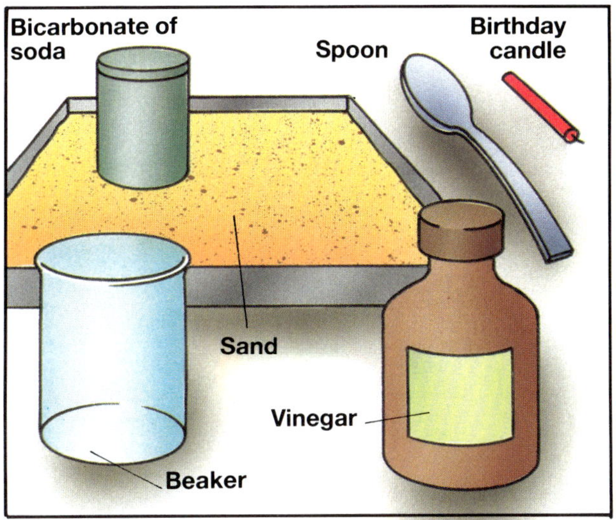

Place a birthday candle in the centre of a tray of sand

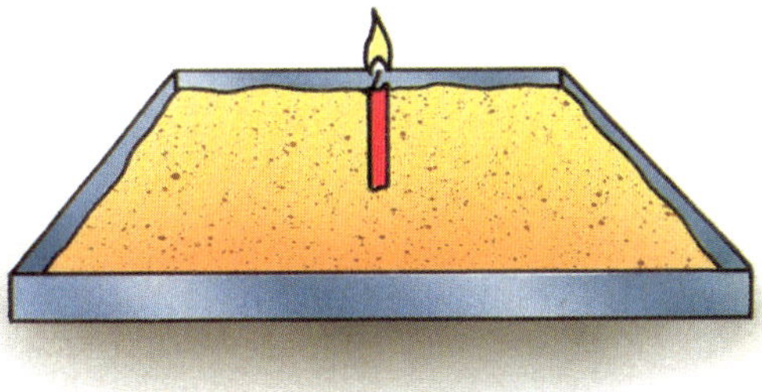

Add a large spoonful of bicarbonate to the beaker of vinegar

You can't see carbon dioxide gas, but because it is heavier than air it pours over the candle flame and smothers it.

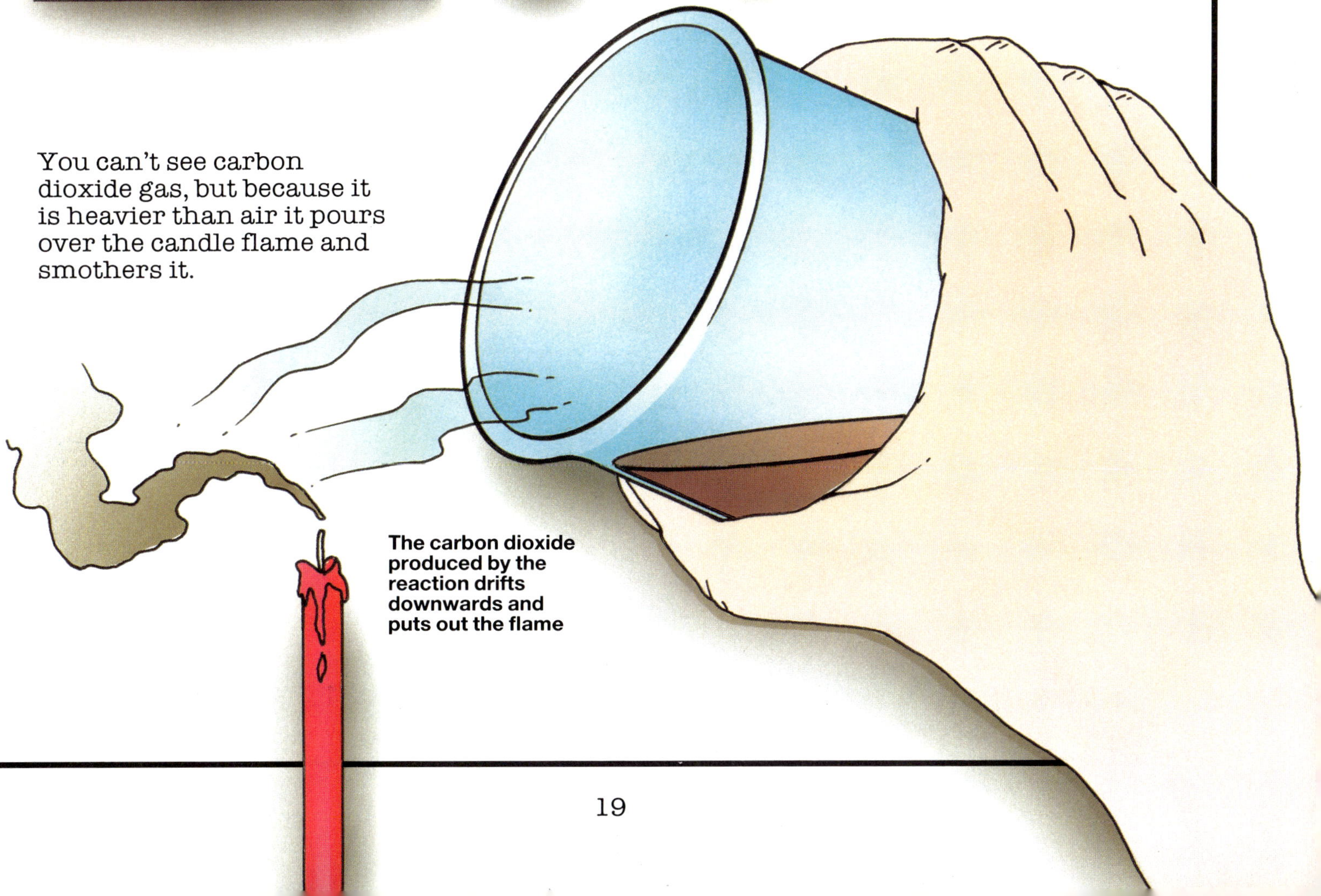

The carbon dioxide produced by the reaction drifts downwards and puts out the flame

GROWING FOOD

Compare the effects of growing seeds under different conditions. Use fast-growing seeds, such as cress, and prepare your samples in exactly the same way. Line the trays with a pad of cotton wool and soak it with the same amount of water, so that it is very damp but not running with excess water. Sprinkle the same quantity of seeds evenly over the cotton wool. Keep one in a warm, sunny position – this is called the control sample. Place a second sample in the same place, but cover the tray with a lid that does not let in light. When the cress in the first tray is growing well, compare the growth with the second sample. What differences do you notice?

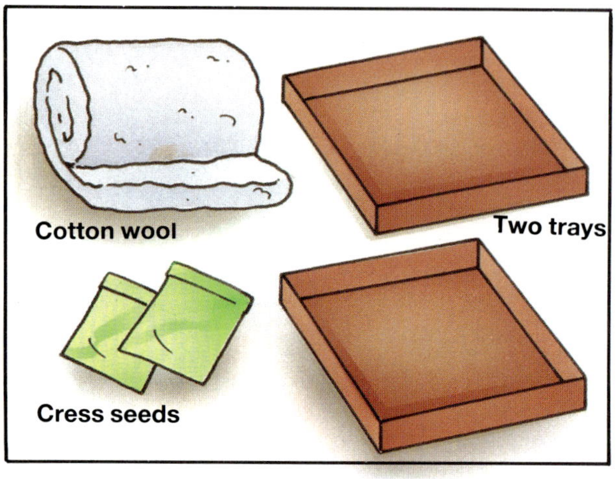

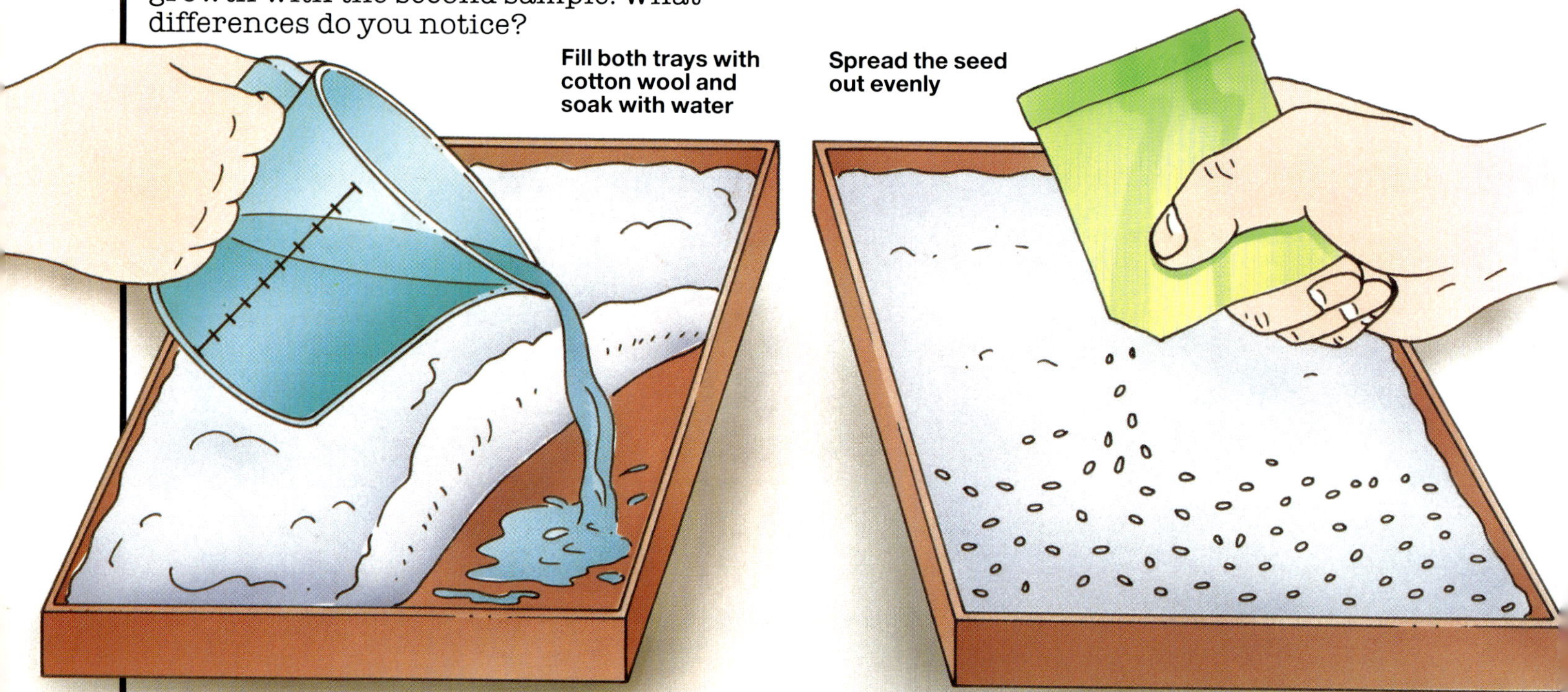

With other samples you can test the effect of pollution on plant growth. Grow one sample using pure water and place it in a warm, sunny position as before. Make up a second tray, but ask an adult to soak the cotton wool in water containing two tablespoons full of bleach. Add a similar amount of washing-up liquid to a third sample. Compare the growth and appearance of the cress plants. What differences do you notice?

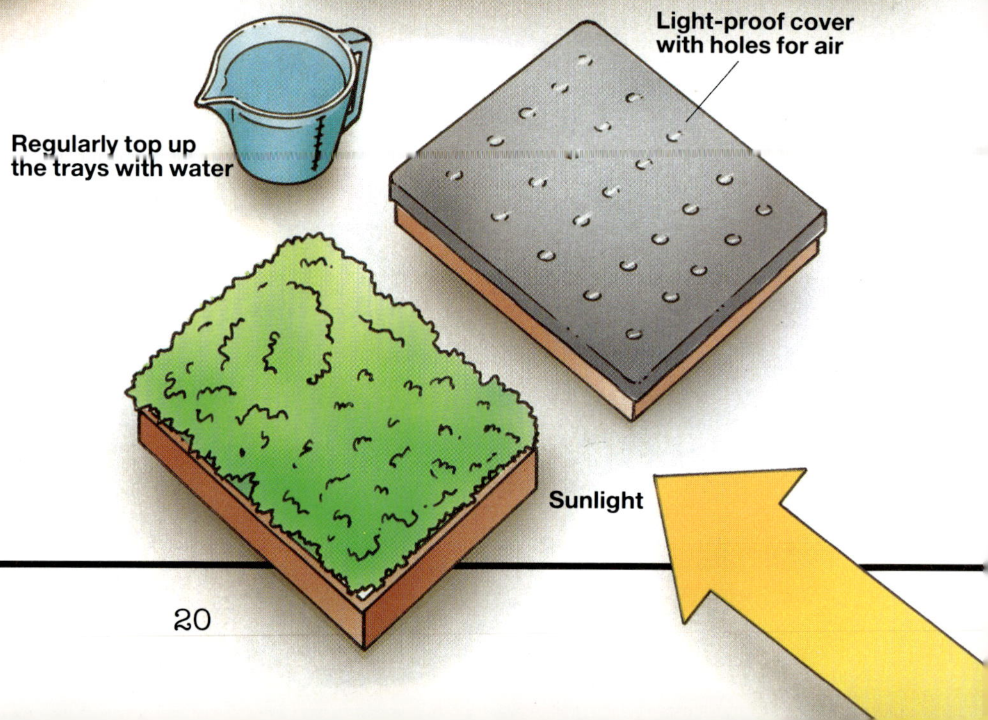

ROTTING

Find several glass, screw-topped jars and place a different sample of food or even some milk into each one. Screw on the lids and seal with sticky tape. Watch the changes that take place over a few weeks. Bacteria in the food causes decay. Because the substances that form may be dangerous, **DO NOT OPEN** the jars. Dispose of them carefully.

RUSTING

Some metals that are left unprotected may begin to rust. Use samples of steel wool or clean iron nails or even dressmakers' pins to see why this happens. Leave one piece of steel wool or some nails or pins in a plastic dish with a little water. Keep the sample damp. In another dish completely cover the wool or nails in water from a kettle that has boiled and then gone cold. Leave a third sample in a dry dish in a warm dry spot. What do you predict will happen to your metal samples?

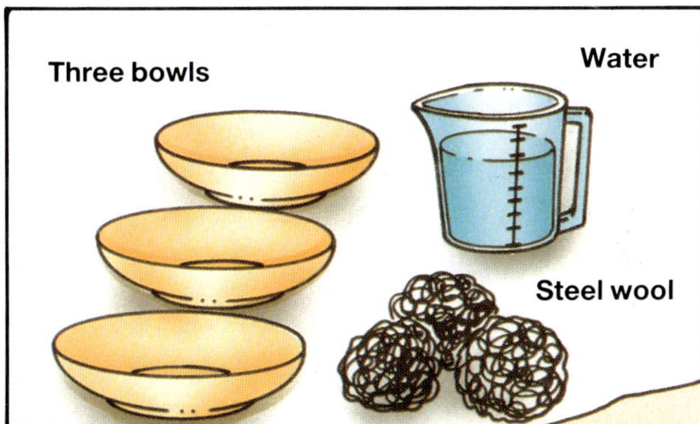

Small amount of water to keep the steel wool damp

To rust, metals need moisture and oxygen. Boiled water has no air, so the sample may not rust. Samples kept damp and open to the air will rust quickly.

Keep this bowl dry

Fill the bowl with water from the kettle so that the steel wool is completely covered

PHYSICS OF HEAT

Heat is a form of energy. Atoms and molecules, the tiny particles that make up everything that exists, are constantly moving and the amount of heat within any substance depends on how much and how fast its atoms move. When more heat energy is given to something its temperature rises, it expands (becomes larger) and it may change from a solid to a liquid or from a liquid to a gas. Heat can be transferred from one place to another in three ways, conduction, convection or radiation, but it can only move from a hotter area to one that has a lower temperature.

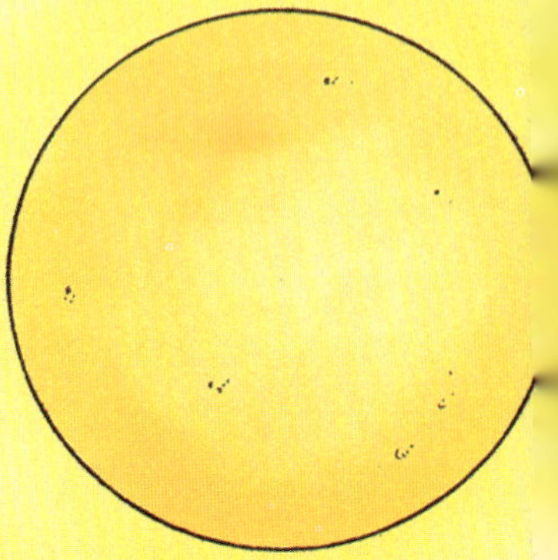

Convection
Hot air rises. The air over a fire, or over an area heated by the Sun, gets hotter and rises, letting colder air flow in below it. Heated water also rises and cooler water flows in to form swirling currents.

Radiation
Nearly all our heat and light come from the Sun. The Sun is 150 million kilometres away, but its heat and light radiation pass through space and reach us at the speed of light eight minutes later.

Conduction
Heat moves through solid objects by conduction. Put a metal spoon in a hot drink and the handle gets warm. The heat around the spoon warms the metal and passes through it along the handle. Some things, like metals, are good heat conductors. Others, called insulators, are not.

PRINCIPLES OF TEMPERATURE

How hot is hot?
Get three bowls with water at different temperatures. Put one hand into a bowl of hot water and the other into cold water. After half a minute put both hands into a bowl of warm water. This water should feel the same to both hands but it doesn't. The cold hand thinks it is in hot water, the hot hand thinks it is in cold water.

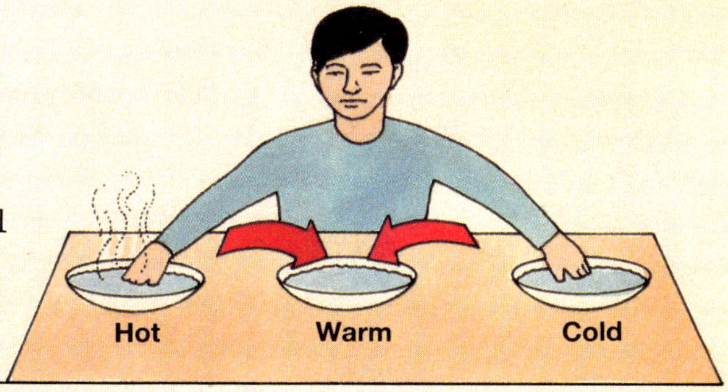

Calibration
Measuring temperatures by touch would mean many mistakes, so we need a standard measure. Liquids, like alcohol and mercury, expand when heated. A thin tube filled with one of these liquids reacts to temperature changes. The tube can be marked at points showing where the liquid expands to when it is heated, and where it contracts to when cooled. The standard temperature points are fixed at the freezing point and boiling point of pure water. The thermometer tube can then be marked at intervals between these fixed points so that it can be used to measure temperatures accurately. Marking a thermometer in this way is called calibration.

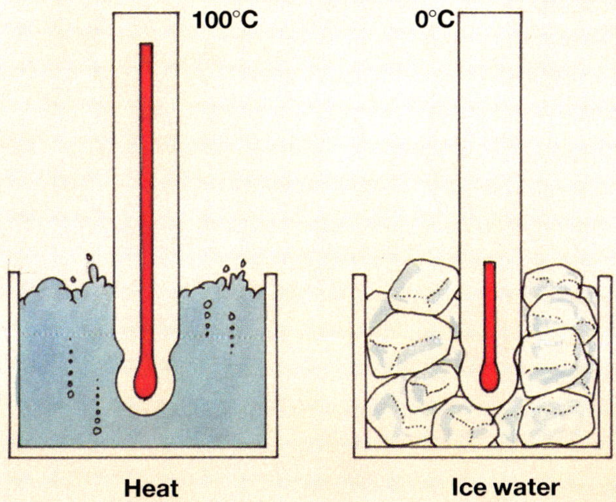

Temperature scales
There are three temperature scales commonly used today. Gabriel Fahrenheit of Germany fixed the freezing point at 32°F and boiling point at 212°F. Anders Celsius of Sweden devised the Celsius scale with 0°C as the freezing point and 100°C as the boiling point. Later a British scientist, William Kelvin, gave us the idea of an absolute zero, the lowest possible temperature, which sets the freezing point of water at 273°K and the boiling point at 373°K. Because it is confusing to have three different scales, the one used most often is the Celsius scale, although many people still use Fahrenheit to describe the weather.

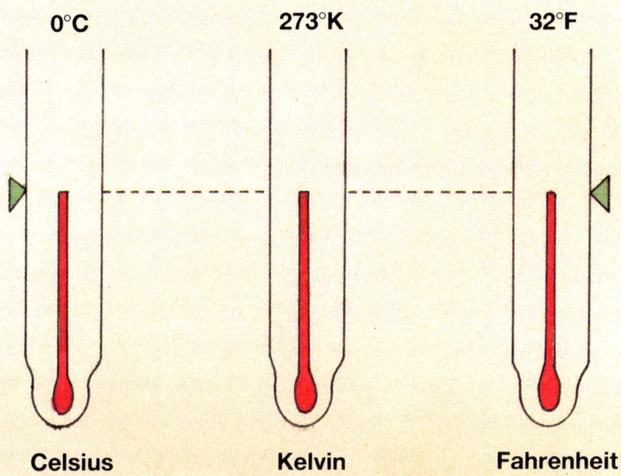

KEEPING WARM

Find four jars with lids and ask an adult to pour hot water of the same temperature into each one. Replace the lids, wrap one jar in a handkerchief, another in a thick woollen scarf and put a third in a box of polystyrene chips or sawdust. Don't wrap the fourth jar. Record the temperature in each jar with a thermometer every half an hour. Which one stays warmest and which one cools fastest?

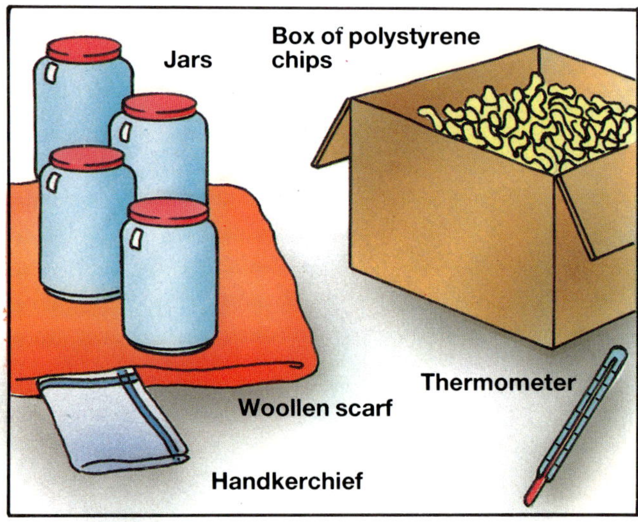

A well wrapped (insulated) jar keeps its heat best. Use this test to compare all kinds of materials to find the best insulators.

Thermos flask
A thermos flask has a sealed double-walled glass container with a vacuum inside. Heat cannot be conducted or convected through a vacuum. Radiated heat is reflected back in by the silvered glass that acts like a mirror. The only heat loss is through the cap, which is well insulated, so hot liquids stay hot for a long time.

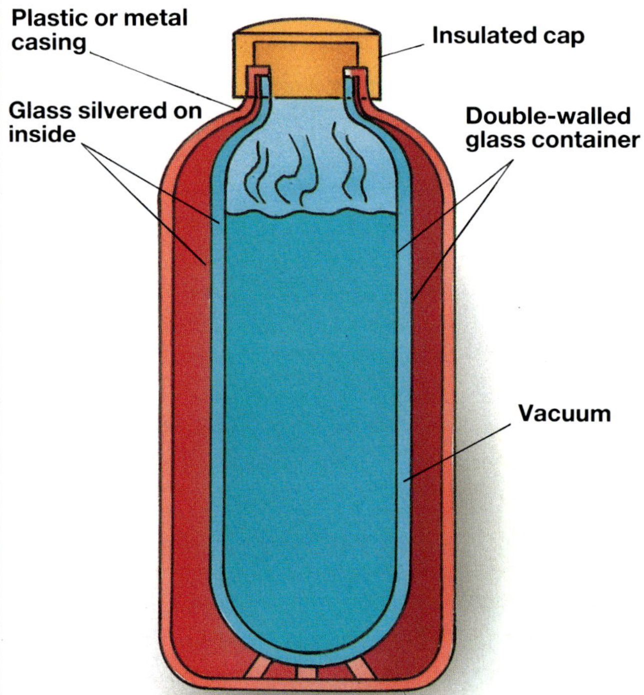

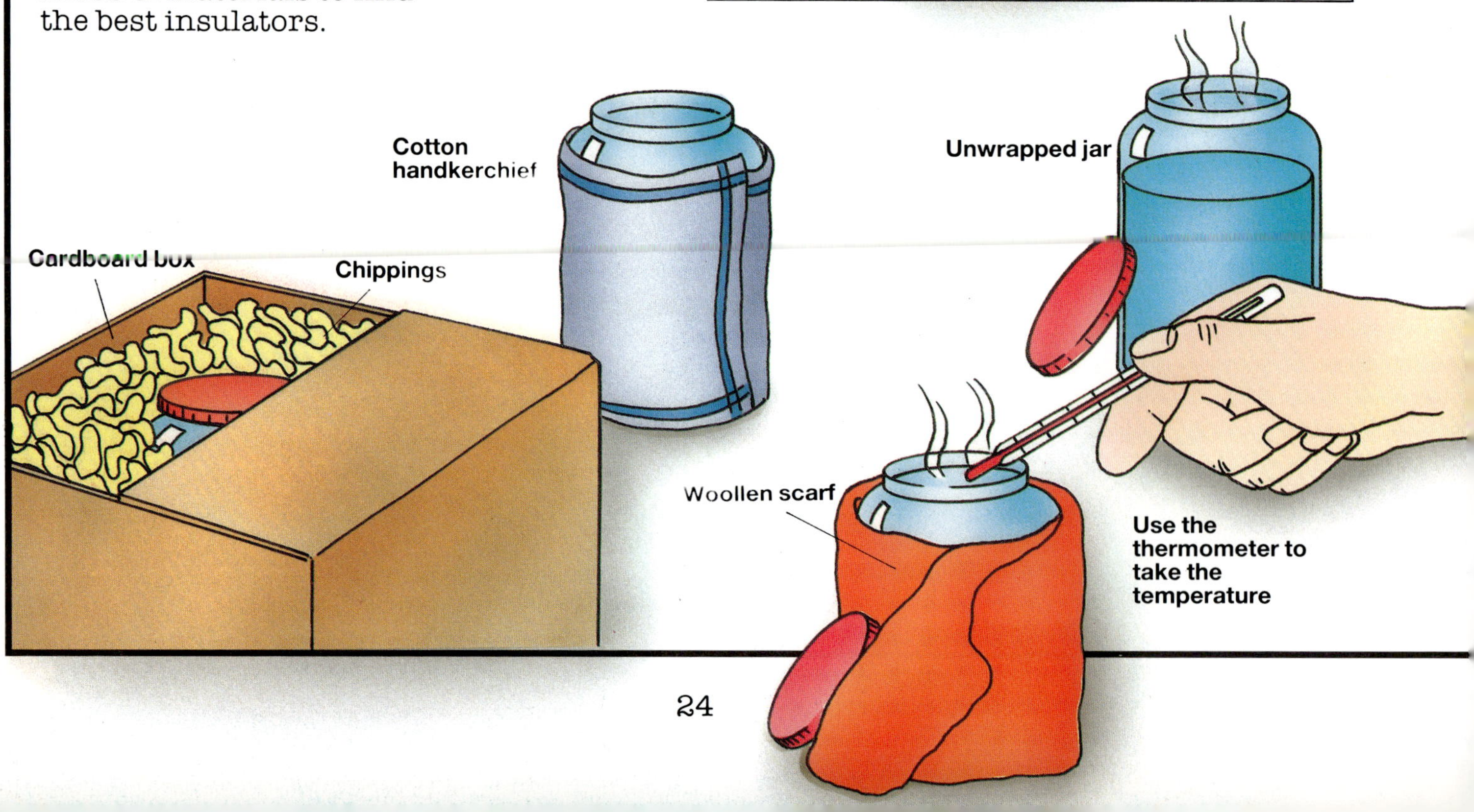

RAISING YOUR CAP

Water is at its most dense, the point where it takes up the smallest amount of space, at a temperature of 4°C. As water freezes into ice it actually expands. This is why water pipes can burst in the winter. Fill a plastic bottle to the very top with cold water. Cover the top with a foil cap and place the bottle upright in a freezer. Leave overnight, then see what has happened. As the water freezes it can only go up.

PUDDLE WATCHING

After a period of heavy rain, find a large puddle and scratch around its edge with a sharp stone, or mark it with chalk. Leave the puddle for about 15 minutes and do the same again. Repeat this four or five times. What do you notice about the puddle? The water seems to be disappearing. But where is it going? Can you estimate how much water disappears during each 15-minute period?

What is happening is that heat from the Sun, helped by wind, makes the water evaporate. You cannot see water vapour in the air, but it is carried into the atmosphere, forming clouds.

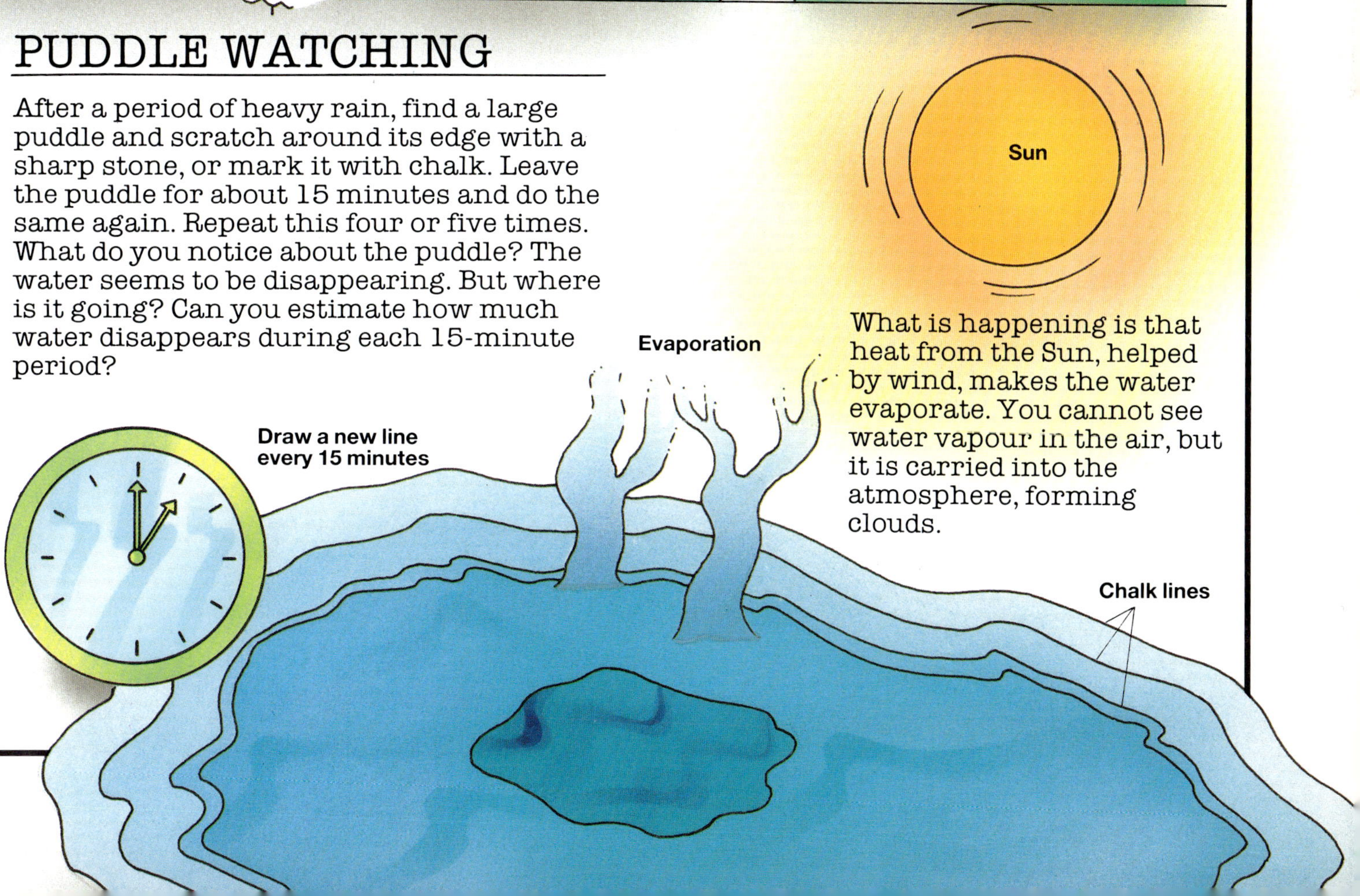

CONVECTION CURRENTS

Put a few drops of ink or food dye in a bottle and fill it with hot water. Cover the top with a foil cap with some thread attached. Lower the bottle into a tank full of clear, cold water. Let the water settle, then pull the foil away, using the thread. Watch as the hot coloured water rises in the tank and swirls around, following the convection currents of cold water flowing in towards the bottle.

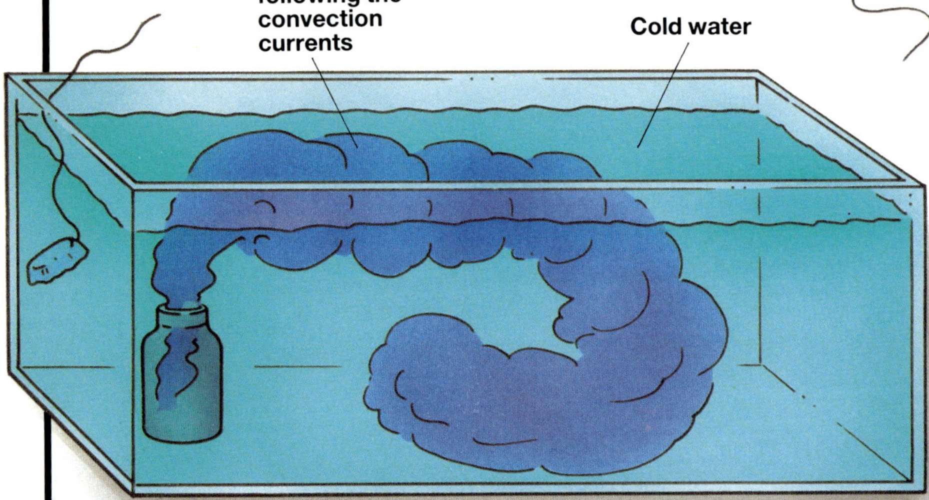

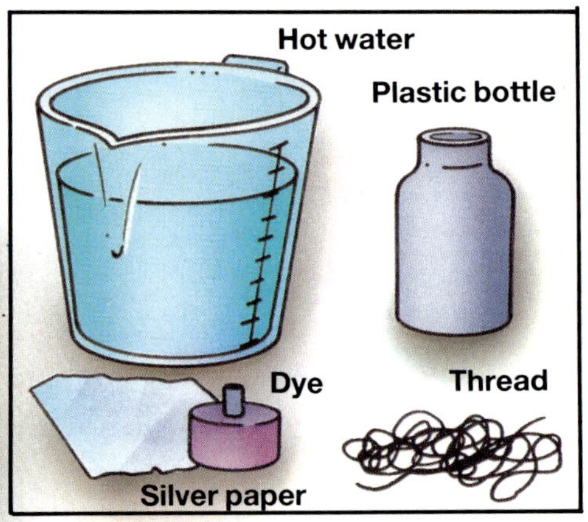

HEAT CONDUCTORS

You can watch the speed with which heat is conducted along a solid object by using candle wax. Ask an adult to help you drip candle wax onto a long nail. Hold the nail with a clothes peg or pair of pliers. Put the end of the nail in a candle flame. As the heat is conducted along the nail the wax begins to melt and drip off.

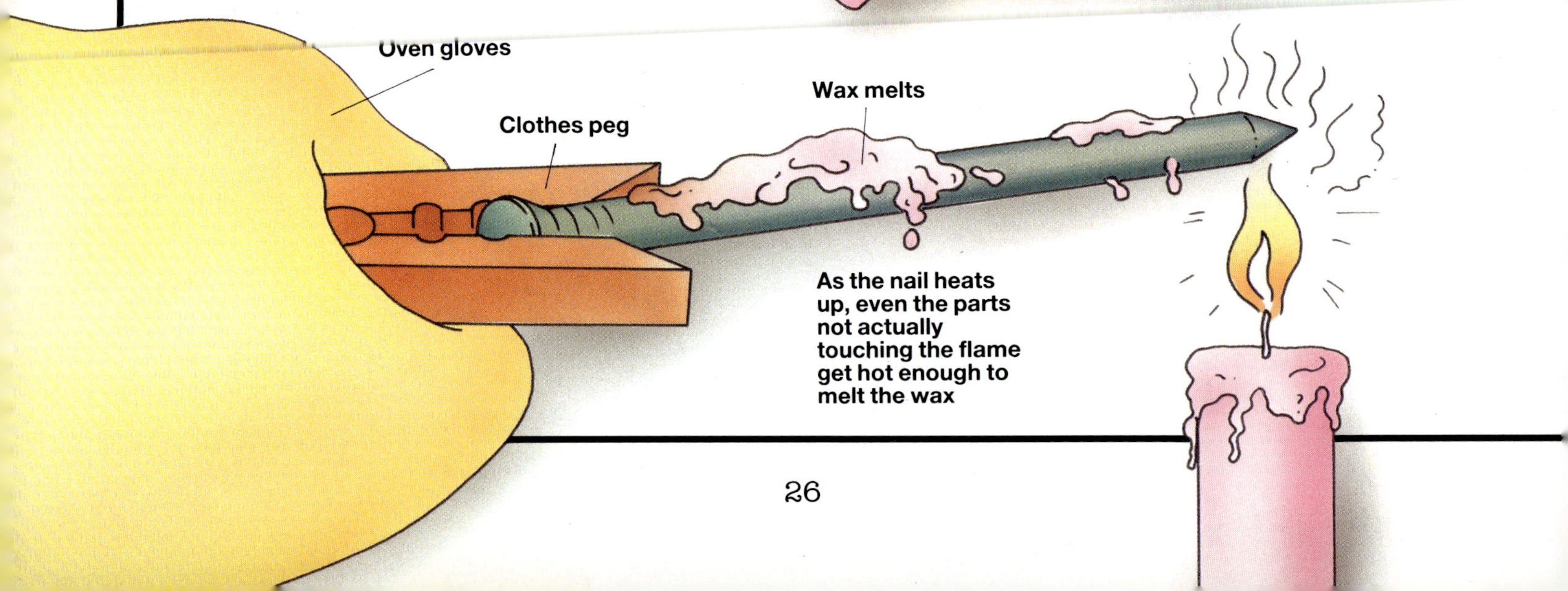

SPIRAL SNAKE

Carefully cut a circle from a sheet of thin paper and cut it into a spiral shape. Hang the spiral from a length of thread over a hot central heating radiator or storage heater. **DO NOT** hang it over a fire or flame. The rising hot air currents catch the spiral, making it twist and turn. In a room, the convection currents that form around a radiator or fire carry the heat all round the room, so that eventually every corner of the room is warmed.

RADIATED HEAT

Radiated heat can be reflected away. Take two identical glass jars, filled with the same amount of cold water. Cover one in black paper and the other in silver foil, then put them in a sunny place for about an hour. Check the temperature. What do you find?

SOURCES OF ENERGY

All of our energy comes from the Sun, whether it is direct heat and light from the Sun's radiated energy, or stored chemical energy in fuels and food. Our problem is that our demand for energy increases every day. Everything in our lives depends on the constant supply of power, particularly electrical power. Think of all the things you use that need electricity to work. Almost every industry needs electrical energy. We use vast quantities of energy. Without it, life as we know it could not continue. So where can all this energy come from?

Gas, coal and oil
We think of fuels as gas, coal and oil. Coal has been important for hundreds of years and oil provides us with petrol and plastics that are in increasing demand. What can we do when these fuels run out?

Wind and water
Waves build up energy as they move across oceans and wind can be powerful enough to uproot trees. Engineers are investigating many interesting ways to harness this natural power, including wave-driven turbines and wind generators.

PRINCIPLES OF SUPPLY

Nuclear power
Scientists discovered that elements such as uranium and plutonium can be used as a source of nuclear energy, giving out vast quantities of heat that could be used destructively in bombs or as a controlled source of energy in nuclear power stations.

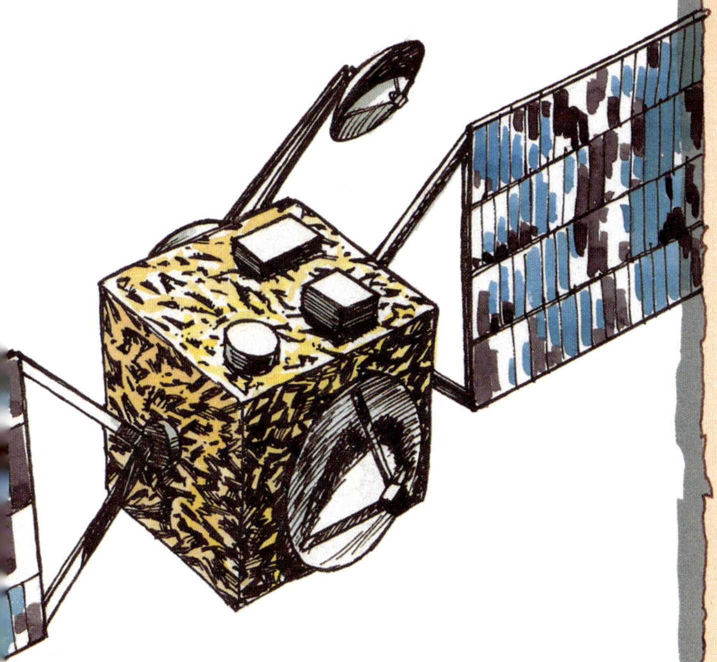

Solar power
In many hot countries, solar panels are used to capture the Sun's heat energy. Water is pumped through a series of pipes laid under a glass panel which is heated by the Sun, giving cheap hot water.

Fossil fuels
Fossil fuels were made over millions of years by the action of pressure and heat upon layers of dead plant and animal tissue under the ground and the sea. Because this process takes so much time, and because we use so much of these fuels to make electricity, Earth's reserves of fossil fuels have almost gone, so we need to develop other sources of power.

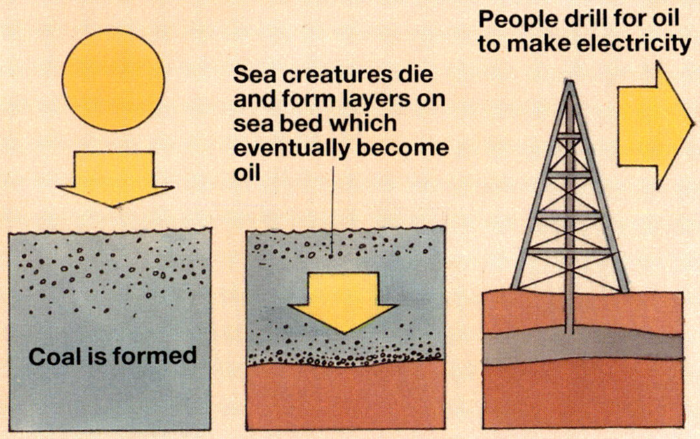

Renewable power
Wind always blows and water constantly flows, providing a free, continuous source of energy. We need to find ways to use this. One that has been used for many years is hydro-electricity. Water trapped behind a dam is released and rushes over turbines, turning them very fast. The turbines are connected to generators that produce electricity.

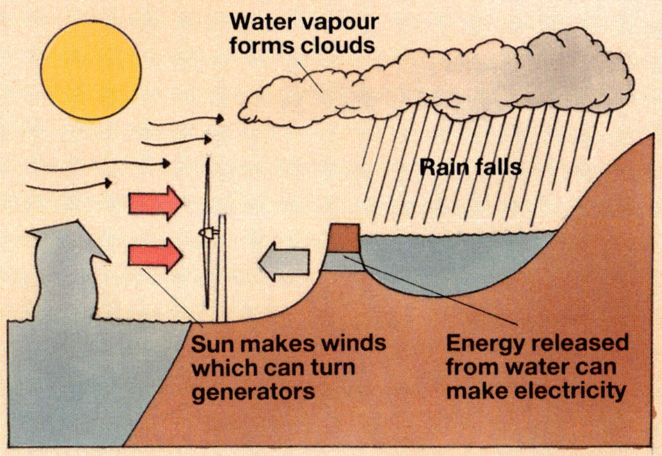

MAKE YOUR OWN WINDMILL

Modern windmills have two or three blades that are specially shaped like an aircraft's wing (an aerofoil shape) to catch the wind and turn at the highest possible speed. The energy that is produced when the blades turn is used to turn a generator that makes electricity. A large wind generator can produce a great deal of electrical power. The windmill shown here turns a little acrobat figure attached to a crank on the windmill blades. Follow the step by step instructions to set your acrobat tumbling.

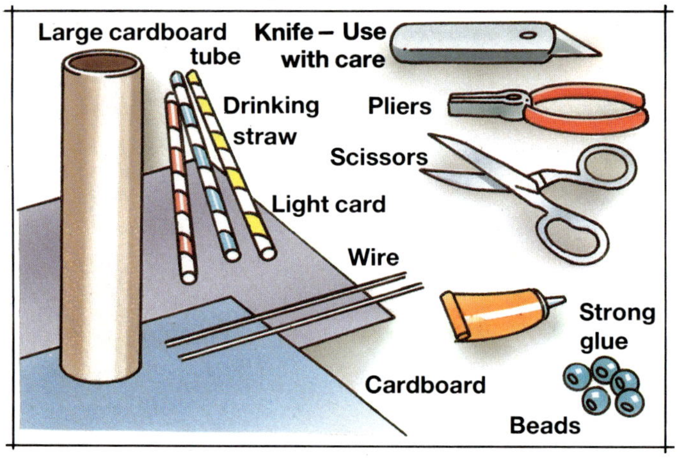

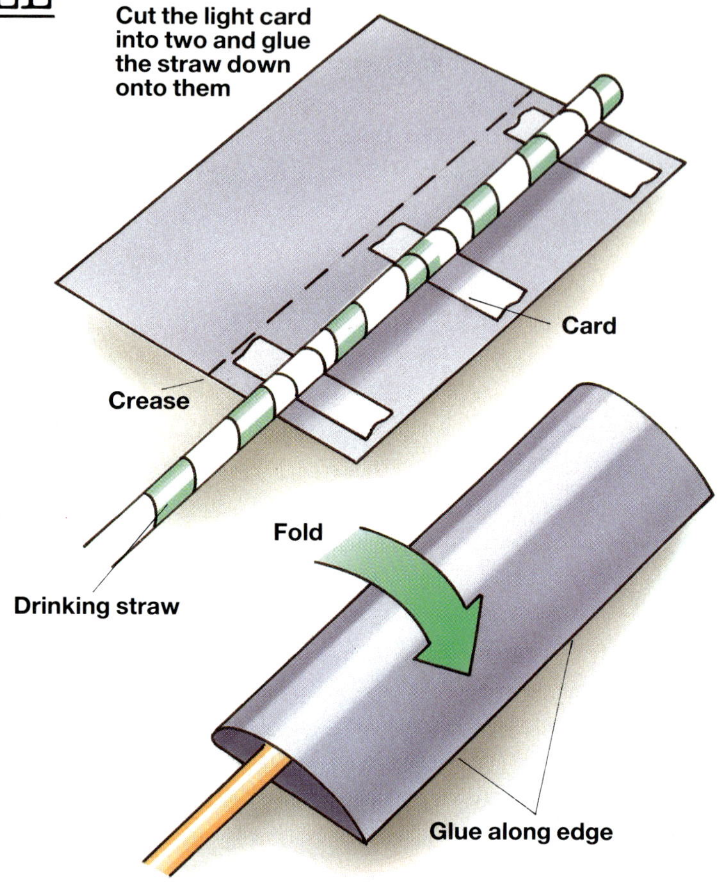

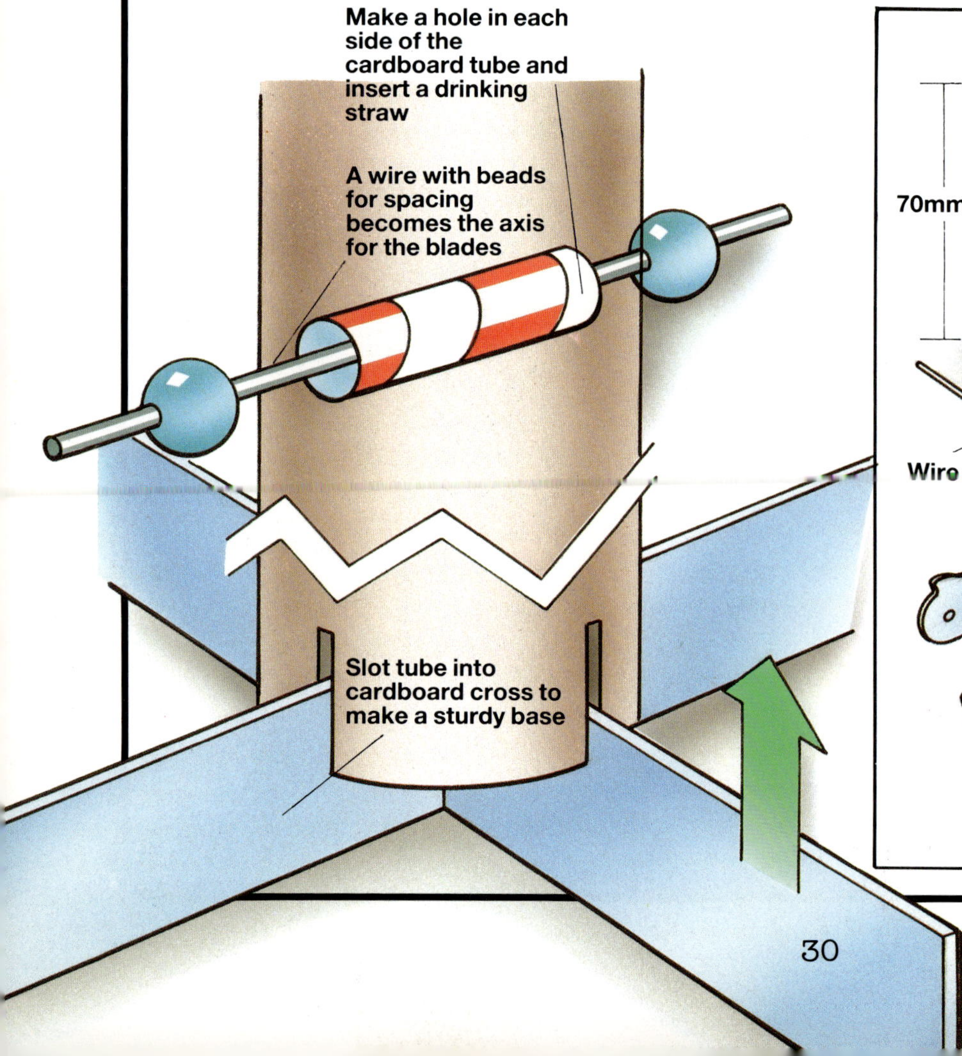

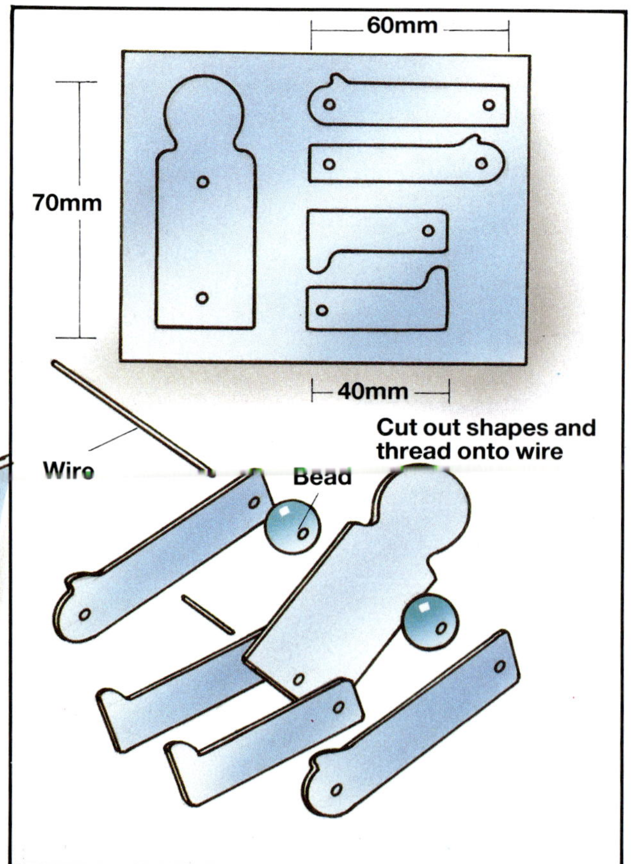

FUTURE ENERGY

Burning fossil fuels can damage our environment by releasing harmful gases. Carbon dioxide released from burning fuels forms a layer in the atmosphere that causes global warming. We need to get more energy from the Sun, wind and waves. We also need to save energy by recycling household waste like glass, metals and paper.

Solar energy

Wave power

Wind power

Geothermal energy

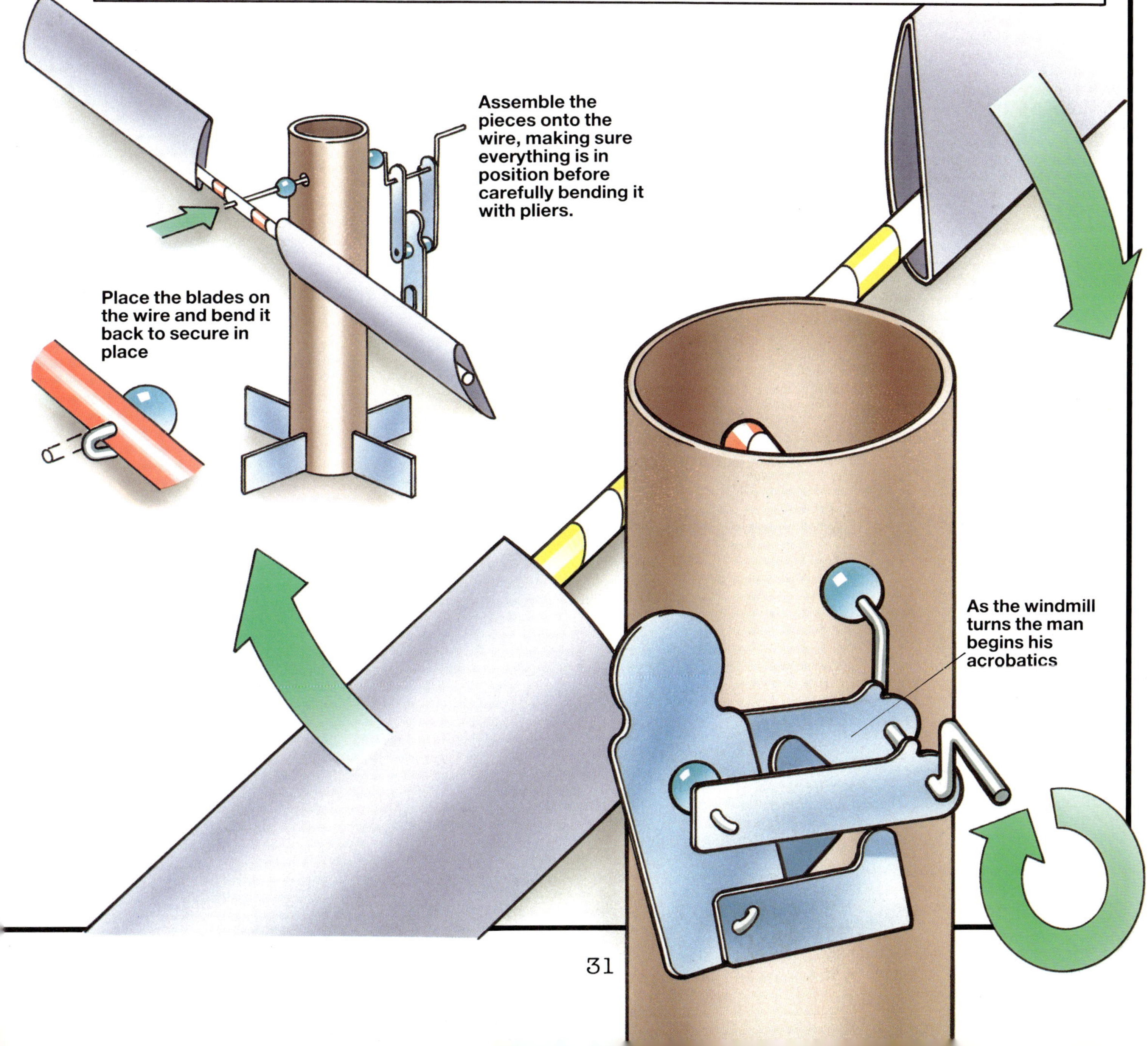

NUCLEAR FISSION

Everything is made from tiny particles called atoms. Some atoms are so large they are unstable and cannot hold together. They break up, giving out a burst of energy and releasing nuclear particles called neutrons. In a large mass of unstable atoms these "free" neutrons can make more atoms break up, creating a continuous reaction called nuclear fission. Early this century it was discovered that some substances like uranium could be made to break up in this way, giving out heat energy that can be used to make electricity. The problem is that this reaction is very dangerous and has to be very carefully controlled. It also leaves large amounts of deadly radioactive waste to be disposed of.

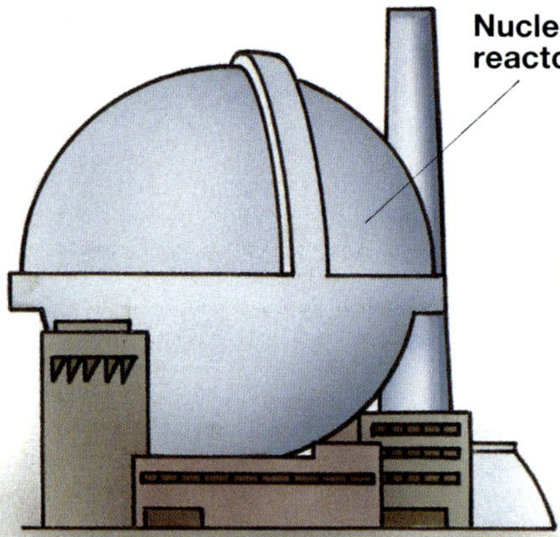

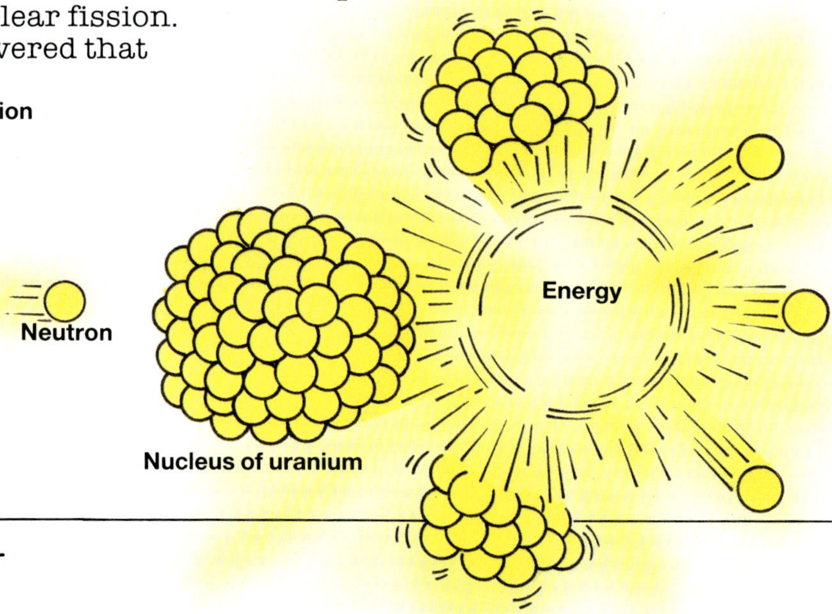

NUCLEAR FUSION

The Sun's energy comes from a process called nuclear fusion. Under very strong heat and pressure, special hydrogen atoms, called deuterium and tritium, combine together to form helium. As this happens, tremendous amounts of heat and light energy are produced. This principle has been used to make nuclear fusion weapons (often called hydrogen bombs) that have terrifying destructive power. Scientists all over the world are trying to find a way to control fusion reactions here on Earth. If they succeed, the energy produced will last us almost for ever. Also, it will not bring any of the current problems that we have with waste polluting the environment, just cheap energy for everyone.

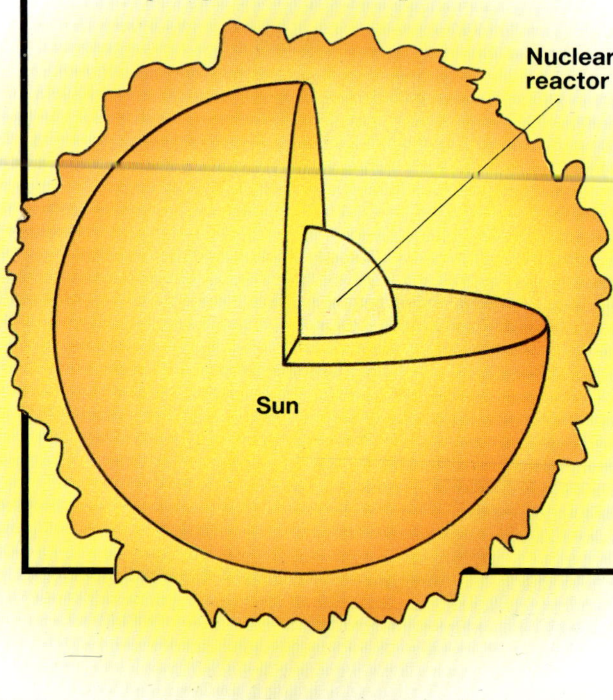

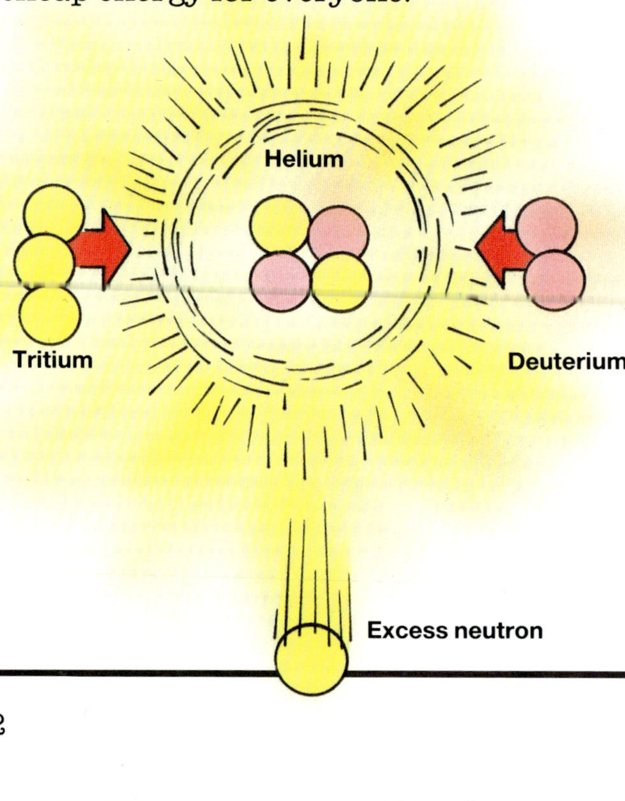